N

O

A

H

N

the *REAL* STORY

O

by LARRY STONE

A

author of *THE STORY OF THE BIBLE*

H

 WND BOOKS

NOAH: THE *REAL* STORY
© 2014 by Lawrence M. Stone

Published by WND Books®, Washington, D.C. WND Books is a registered trademark of WorldNetDaily.com, Inc. ("WND")

Unless otherwise indicated, all Scripture quotations are from The Holy Bible, English Standard Version® (ESV®), copyright © 2001 by Crossway, a publishing ministry of Good News Publishers. Used by permission. All rights reserved.

Scripture quotations marked GNT are from the Good News Translation in Today's English Version—Second Edition Copyright © 1992 by American Bible Society. Used by Permission.

Scripture quotations from *THE MESSAGE* copyright © by Eugene H. Peterson 1993, 1994, 1995, 1996, 2000, 2001, 2002. Used by permission of NavPress Publishing Group.

Scripture quotations marked NIV are taken from the Holy Bible, New International Version®. Copyright © 1973, 1978, 1984, 2011 by Biblica, Inc.TM Used by permission of Zondervan. All rights reserved worldwide. www.zondervan.com. The "NIV" and "New International Version" are trademarks registered in the United States Patent and Trademark Office by Biblica, Inc.TM

Scripture taken from the New King James Version® (NKJV) copyright © 1982 by Thomas Nelson, Inc. Used by permission. All rights reserved.

Scripture quotations from King James Version are marked KJV.

WND Books are distributed to the trade by:
Midpoint Trade Books, 27 West 20th Street, Suite 1102, New York, New York 10011

WND Books are available at special discounts for bulk purchases. WND Books, Inc., also publishes books in electronic formats. For more information call (541) 474-1776 or visit www.wndbooks.com

Paperback ISBN: 978-1-936488-74-2

Typesetting by Natasha Fondren, the eBook Artisans
Maps created by Bill Kersey, Kersey Graphics, Nashville, Tennessee
Cover designed by Mark Karis

Library of Congress Catalog-in-Publication Data Available Upon Request
Printed in the United States of America

14 15 16 17 18 19 EBM 9 8 7 6 5 4 3 2 1

CONTENTS

Introduction   I

1. Noah and His Floating Zoo   9
2. Flood Stories around the World   21
3. Water, Water Everywhere   35
4. How Big Was the Ark?   49
5. The Animals Went in Two by Two   61
6. Ararat: The Mountain of Pain   83
7. Arkaeologists: Searching for the Ark   97
8. Noah Goes to Hollywood   III
9. Where Can You See the Ark?   125
10. Noah's Secret for Surviving the End of the World   137

Notes   151

ILLUSTRATIONS

"Noah's Ark," by Edward Hicks (1846)   14
Manu and seven rishis are saved from the great flood   25
Nanabozho   28
Noah and the ark from a Flemish manuscript   34
Bill of sale from Shuruppak   37
The Turkish Straits (map)   41
Pangaea (map)   44
Noah's ark, from the *Nuremberg Chronicle* (1493)   48
Edge-jointed planking   52
A model of the ark   54
Comparison of ship sizes   58
Noah's ark, by Elfred Lee   60
Page from *An Essay towards a Real Character
  and a Philosophical Language* (1668)   67
Sloped floor and manure gutter   77
Mount Ararat, the Mountain of Pain   82
Great Ararat and Little Ararat   85
Mount Ararat, Mount Judi, and Mount Suleiman   92
Page from *The Chicago Tribune*, August 10, 1883   98
Fernand Navarra holds a piece of wood   103
Page from *Life Magazine*, September 5, 1960   108
"That woodpecker has to go." (cartoon)   110
Poster for *Noah's Ark* (1928)   115

Poster for *Evan Almighty* (2007)   118
Noah's Ark Park and Resort, Hong Kong   124
Johan's Ark, Dordrecht, Holland   126
Ark Encounter, Williamstown, Kentucky   133

To Lois

An excellent wife, a caring mother, an adoring grandmother, a lover of flowers, music, nature, and all things beautiful. With gratitude for your patience, understanding, and support through floods and many adventures.

NOAH

THE *REAL* STORY

INTRODUCTION

"I'm gonna make it rain for a thousand days and drown 'em right out," said God, according to comedian Bill Cosby.

"Listen," Noah told God. "Save water. Let it rain for forty days and forty nights and wait for the sewers to back up."

Noah and the ark makes it on everyone's list of top ten favorite Bible stories—right up there with Jonah and the whale, and David and Goliath. God commanded Noah to build an ark to save his family and animals from a flood that would cover "all the high mountains." When the waters receded, the ark rested "on the mountains of Ararat," Noah opened the door, let the animals out, built an altar, and worshipped God. God promised He would never again destroy the earth with a flood and gave the rainbow as a sign of that promise.

In retrospect, it's easy to say Noah was a hero. He saved animals and his family from the most devastating flood the earth has ever known.

But at the time he must have seemed to be a bit of a nut. He spent sixty to eighty years building a 450-foot-long boat in his backyard. He collected enough food for thousands of animals for a year. And then the animals showed up. What would you think if your neighbor did that? And if your neighbor said God was going to destroy the earth with a flood, how would you react? Would you believe him or call the municipal codes department to get the animals out of your neighborhood?

Noah was probably not the first and certainly has not been the last person to be laughed at for an unpopular idea. Galileo spent the last eight years of his life under house arrest for supporting the crazy idea that the earth revolves around the sun instead of what most people thought at the time—the sun revolves around the earth. When Alexander Graham Bell offered his patent for a telephone to what later became Western Union, a company committee said, "The idea of installing 'telephones' in every city is idiotic.... (This) ungainly and impractical device...has too many shortcomings to be seriously considered as a means of communication." And when Steve Wozniak invented the personal computer, his employer, Hewlett-Packard, saw no future in it. Ken Olson, founder of Digital Equipment Corporation—at the time the second largest manufacturer of computers—said, "There is no reason anyone would want a computer in their home." So Steve Wozniak and Steve Jobs created the Apple computer. Galileo, Alexander Graham Bell, and Steve Wozniak were all told they were wrong. But it turns out they were right.

Noah believed what God had told him. And even though the experts and his neighbors thought he was nutty, he took action. It's easy in retrospect to say he was a hero, but it was not so easy at the time.

Probably no story in the Bible has raised as many questions and has generated as much controversy as Noah and the ark. The story in the Bible is just the beginning!

- Who was Noah?
- How big was the ark?
- Did the Flood cover the whole earth?
- How many animals were on the ark?

And the big question...the one about which books have been written, movies made, and television programs broadcast...

- Where is the ark now?

For thousands of years, people have said the ark is on Mount Ararat in eastern Turkey, and hundreds of people—from St. Jacob in the fourth century, to a Dutch sailor in the eighteenth century, to a U.S. astronaut in the twentieth—have all searched for it.

This is the story of Noah, the Flood, the animals, the ark, and those who have looked for it.

In the twentieth and twenty-first centuries we have retold the story in film, on stage (complete with live animals), and "Captain Noah" has been a television star. We have built replicas of the ark in Holland, Hong Kong, and Canada. Noah-and-the-ark theme parks are planned for Kentucky and Florida.

The Bible says the ark saved people and animals when the world as they knew it was destroyed. How can we save ourselves in the event of a future destruction of the earth? Interestingly, the Bible says the story of Noah and the ark also holds a "secret" to how to survive the end of the world.

Until about two hundred fifty years ago, few people questioned the supernatural stories of the Bible—Jesus' feeding five thousand with five loaves and two fish, Moses leading Israelites across the Red Sea, and the creation of the world in six days. Scientists, geologists, and early paleontologists approached their scientific discovery with the assumption that Noah's Flood explained how the world was shaped. They interpreted evidence they found through the lens of what they believed to be true—the Bible.

Geologist David Montgomery explains.

Today, geologists generally dismiss Noah's Flood with a chuckle and shrug it off as a relic of another time. But for centuries it was considered common knowledge among Christians and many natural philosophers that Noah's Flood shaped our world. What else could have?…Geologists tend to forget that the foundation of modern geology, [seventeenth century bishop and scientist Nicholas] Steno's deceptively simple idea that younger rocks lay on top of older ones, was introduced to help explain how Noah's Flood shaped the Italian landscape. Yet Steno's story remains one of the best examples of the complex interplay between geology and theology…. The

more natural philosophers applied Steno's rules to the geologic record, the more they discovered about how the rocks
revealed a much longer story than the traditional biblically-
inspired history of the world."[1]

The discoveries suggesting "a much longer story" brought
about a change in the scientific community's thinking about
the Flood. Thomas Huxley, an English biologist and influential
advocate of Darwin's theory of evolution, explains.

At the present time [1893], it is difficult to persuade serious
scientific inquirers to occupy themselves, in any way, with
the Noachian Deluge. They look at you with a smile and a
shrug, and say they have more important matters to attend
to.... But it was not so in my youth. At that time, geologists
and biologists could hardly follow to the end of any path of
inquiry without finding the way blocked by Noah and his
ark, or by the first chapter of Genesis; and it was a serious
matter, in this country at any rate, for a man to be suspected
of doubting the literal truth of the Diluvial...history.[2]

Henry Morris and John Whitcomb, authors of *The Genesis
Flood*, also recount the recent history of the interplay between
geology and the Bible as it concerns the Flood.

The Flood was once believed to be the explanation for
most of the phenomena of geology; later it was regarded
as one of a series of geological cataclysms which were the
key features of geologic interpretation; then it was thought
to explain only certain of the superficial deposits of the

earth's surface; finally it was either dismissed as legendary or interpreted as a local flood in Mesopotamia, thus stripping it of all geological consequence.[3]

The events in the story of Noah are not as obviously "a violation of the laws of nature" (the definition of a miracle given by philosopher David Hume in the 1700s) as Jesus' walking on water was. But when you start looking at details of the story, there are many miraculous elements that are quite difficult to explain.

Morris and Whitcomb's 1961 book drew a line in the sand, widening the divide between science and the Bible. Previously the tension had tended to be a more healthy one. Seven years before Whitcomb and Morris's book, Bernard Ramm, a seminary professor, wrote *The Christian View of Science and Scripture*, calling for a return to "the tradition of late nineteenth-century conservative scholars, who learned the facts of science and Scripture with patience, care and integrity, and showed with great competence and training that these two can never conflict."[4]

Instead of accepting the Bible and scientific discovery as telling the same story of the earth's formation from different viewpoints, the two sides hardened. "Either the Biblical record of the Flood is false and must be rejected or else the system of historical geology which has seemed to discredit it is wrong and must be changed. The latter alternative would seem to be the only one which a biblically and scientifically instructed Christian could honestly take,"[5] said Morris and Whitcomb. Ken Ham, founder of Answers in Genesis, upped the ante: "What is at stake is the authority of all of God's Word. Indeed, if the text of Scripture in Genesis 6–8 clearly teaches that the Flood was global and we reject that teaching, then we undermine the reliability and authority of other parts of Scripture, including John 3:16."[6] That doesn't leave much room for discussion.

Author Robert Moore's comment, "the story of the Great Flood and the voyage of the ark, as expounded by modern creationists...cannot possibly be accepted by any thinking person,"[7] doesn't leave much room for discussion either. It comes close to name-calling. The introduction to Moore's article also cuts off conversation: "Knowledgeable people are well aware that Genesis 1 through 11 is not scientific or historical but largely mythical, metaphorical, poetic, theological, and moral. All people are not knowledgeable, however."[8]

This great divide has interesting ramifications for a book about Noah, the ark, the animals, and the Flood. For instance, if we ask how Noah and his family could have fed and provided water for all the animals on the ark, we will not get an answer from someone on the no-thinking-person-can-believe-it side of the divide. They don't have to come up with an answer. Noah never took care of animals on an ark that never existed.

Instead, we have to ask our questions of someone on the this-is-the-only-way-a-Christian-can-believe side of the divide. They are committed to explaining the feasibility of Noah's ark and have spent a lot of time figuring it out.

1.
NOAH AND HIS FLOATING ZOO

Everyone knows about Noah and the ark. The story has been the subject of mystery plays in the Middle Ages, of movies from a partly silent film in 1928 to Darren Aronofsky's 2014 epic, and of television shows such as *Captain Noah and His Magical Ark*. Noah and the ark have been the subject of board games, toys, children's books, and nursery wallpaper. And there are even a handful of theme parks built around Noah and the ark.

In San Antonio, Texas, is an ordinary-looking white brick Sunday school building. But inside the two-story structure at the 19,000-member Cornerstone Church is a fun Noah's-Ark-inspired children's activity building. A lion, an elephant, a talking macaw, and six other animals are animatronic, meaning they move. A giraffe stands in the middle of a two-story central hall. The rhinoceros previously appeared in a John Cusack movie. Children can play on a giant Galapagos tortoise.

• • •

But what do we really know about Noah? Not much that we can say for sure.

Noah was the grandson of Methuselah, the oldest man in the Bible, and father of Ham, Shem, and Japheth. We don't know when Noah lived, but estimates range from 5,500 BC to 2,300 BC, putting him squarely in the Neolithic Period—the last part of the Stone Age when metal tools were becoming widespread, agriculture was developing, and humans began to domesticate animals.

Noah is remembered for having built an ark in preparation for a Great Flood that destroyed the world, with only Noah, his family, and a boatload of animals being saved. It's a story told in the Bible and in the Quran. And similar stories are found throughout the world.

The Statler Brothers recounted the beginning of the Bible's Noah story pretty well.

The Lord looked down from His window in the sky,
Said, "I created man, but I don't remember why.
Nothing but fighting since creation day.
I'll send a little water and wash 'em all away."

The Lord came down to look around a spell,
And there was Mister Noah behaving mighty well,
And that is the reason, the Scriptures record,
That Noah found grace in the eyes of the Lord.[9]

Wickedness was rampant on the earth. How bad was it? There was violence, sexual immorality, corruption, and widespread lawlessness. People ignored God; He wasn't even on their radar screen. "Human evil was out of control. People thought evil, imagined evil—evil, evil, evil from morning to night."[10]

The Bible is clear that God was upset with the wickedness on the earth, sorry He had made people, and was ready to destroy humans, animals, and birds with a flood. But between the first mention of Noah and the story of the Flood are four strange verses that seem to explain the wickedness on the earth. But what they mean is not very clear.

The Bible says, "the sons of God saw that the daughters of man were attractive. And they took as their wives any they chose."

Who were the sons of God? Those who study the Bible have three suggestions: (1) godly descendants of Seth, the third son of Adam and Eve; (2) angels; (3) kings and rulers (for instance, later Egyptian kings were called the son of Re, the sun god).

Who were the daughters of man? For the first suggestion, the daughters of man are considered to be ungodly descendants of Seth's brother, Cain. For the second and third suggestions, the daughters of man are said to be sexually attractive women.

The Bible then says, "The Nephilim were on the earth in those days, and also afterward, when the sons of God came in to the daughters of man and they bore children to them. These were the mighty men who were of old, the men of renown." *Nephilim* is a Hebrew word many translate as "giants." Some say these giants were not just big in size, but also savage and violent attackers who pillaged the earth…not the kind of person you would want to invite home to meet your mother.

However, an ancient Jewish book said to be written by Enoch, the great-grandfather of Noah, may give us a clue. The Book of Enoch, which has not been generally accepted as Scripture, says 200 angels in heaven saw the beautiful daughters of men, lusted after them, and took them as wives and they gave birth to giants. These angels taught humans how to work in metal and make swords and knives. They taught humans about enchantments and how to read the signs of the sun and the moon. "And there arose much godlessness, and they committed fornication, and they were led astray, and became corrupt in all their ways." These fallen angels, called Watchers, were then bound until the Judgment Day.[11]

It's not clear by just reading these verses—Genesis 6:1-4— what is going on. Whatever it is, though, the Bible is clear: "Human evil was out of control."

But Noah was different. He was a good man, a man of integrity.

According to the same Book of Enoch, Noah's father, Lamech, was frightened by baby Noah's angelic appearance—his radiant face, his white hair, his rosy skin, his praising God—and so Lamech asked his father, Methuselah, for advice. Methuselah went to *his* father, Enoch, who predicted Noah "will be righteous and blameless.... He and his sons will be saved from the corruption of the earth and from all sinners and from all iniquities that are consummated upon the earth in his days."[12]

God spoke to Noah and said that He was going to destroy every living thing on earth with a flood, but Noah should build an ark (we don't know what the word in Hebrew means) out of gopher wood (we don't know what the word in Hebrew means) and cover it inside and out with pitch (we don't know what the word in Hebrew means). God told Noah how big to make the ark, and to make it with three decks and rooms inside and an opening at the top and a door in the side. Once Noah finished building the ark, God said, he should take into it his wife, his three sons and their wives, and a male and female of every kind of "unclean" air-breathing land animal. He should also take seven pairs of ritually "clean" animals and birds. And he should take enough food for the people and the animals.

The Bible does not record any words spoken by Noah before the Flood. However, the Quran, which tells essentially the same story, says Noah preached to anyone who would listen, warning them of the coming flood: "O my people! Worship God! You have no other god but Him. I fear for you the punishment of a dreadful day!"[13] Jewish legend says that for 120 years Noah urged people to change their ways and warned that God would send a flood if they did not. Evidently no one listened to him.

Noah, his family, and the animals boarded the ark, God shut the door, and seven days later, "all the outlets of the vast body of water beneath the earth burst open, all the floodgates of the sky were opened, and rain fell on the earth for forty days and nights."[14] The floodwaters rose until "all the high mountains under the whole heaven were covered" and everything not on the ark died: "Birds, farm animals, wild animals, the entire teeming exuberance of life—dead. And all people—dead."[15] The floodwaters covered the earth for about five months.

As the water began to go down, the ark came to rest "on the mountains of Ararat." Noah opened a window and sent out

Noah's Ark, 1846, by Edward Hicks, an American painter and Quaker preacher. Calmness and peace characterize this idealistic painting, as they did many of Hicks's paintings. (Wikipedia)

a raven, which flew around looking for land. Noah then sent out a dove, which could not find a place to land either and came back to the safety of the ark. A week later Noah again sent out a dove, which this time came back with an olive leaf in its beak, indicating the water was subsiding. After another week, Noah sent out the dove once more and this time it didn't come back.

One year and ten days after the flood unleashed its fury on the earth, God told Noah to leave the ark and take all the animals with him. The ark was a huge ship and Noah and his family had probably kept busy taking care of the animals, although they might have also played a lot of Senet or Mehen (ancient board games). But after a year they were undoubtedly glad to disembark onto solid land.

The first thing Noah did was to build an altar and make a sacrifice of clean animals and birds. God then promised, "never again will everything living be destroyed by floodwaters; no, never again will a flood destroy the earth."[16]

For as long as earth lasts,
    planting and harvest, cold and heat,
Summer and winter, day and night
    will never stop.[17]

The sign of God's promise was the rainbow. Every time there is a rainbow, God said, He would remember His covenant with humans and every living thing, and never again would flood-waters destroy all life on earth.

When Noah's family left the ark, they were the only eight people left alive on the earth. God said,

Whoever sheds human blood,
    by humans let his blood be shed,
Because God made humans in his image
    reflecting God's very nature.
You're here to bear fruit, reproduce,
    lavish life on the earth, live bountifully![18]

Traditionally, it was thought that everyone on earth was descended from Noah's three sons. "From these the whole earth was populated,"[19] the Bible says. Ham was said to be the father of southern people—Africans and the Canaanites. Shem was said to be the father of the middle people—Jews and Arabs; the term "Semitic" is still used today. Japheth was said to be the father of northern people—European or Caucasian people. Asian people have been attributed to each of Noah's three sons by different scholars.

There are parallels between Adam and Noah. Both Adam and Noah were founders of new races. Adam was the father of humankind; Noah was the father of all people after the Flood. Both Adam and Noah were righteous when we first meet them. Adam's sin led him and his wife to be expelled from the Garden of Eden. Noah's sin and that of his son Ham occurred after the Flood.

The last story about Noah is not usually found in Bible storybooks. Noah planted a vineyard, made wine, became drunk, and lay naked in his tent. His son Ham, the father of Canaan, saw the nakedness of his father and told his two brothers, who walked in backwards and put a garment over Noah. Noah cursed Canaan, the son of Ham, saying, "and may Canaan be his (Shem's) servant."

The story of Noah's drunkenness is in stark contrast to the description of him before the Flood as being a righteous man.

Commentators do not agree on how to interpret this story. Was it told to justify the Israelites' taking the Canaanite lands and subjugating the people? What was the real sin of Ham? Was it just seeing Noah? Or was it telling others of Noah's drunkenness and mocking him? Was Ham's sin in having sex with Noah's wife? All of these have been suggested in an effort to explain the curse Noah put on the son of Ham—a curse that is difficult to justify with only the information given in the Bible.

And even though there is nothing here to indicate race, "the curse of Ham" was later interpreted by some Jews, Christians, and Muslims as being a curse on people of black skin and used to justify slavery. This interpretation became more common in the eighteenth and nineteenth centuries when there was an active slave trade.

"I understand that there are Christians among you who try to justify segregation on the basis of the Bible," said Martin Luther King in 1956. "They argue that the Negro is inferior by nature because of Noah's curse upon the children of Ham. Oh my friends, this is blasphemy. This is against everything that the Christian religion stands for. I must say to you as I have said to so many Christians before, that in Christ 'there is neither Jew nor Gentile, there is neither bond nor free, there is neither male nor female, for we are all one in Christ Jesus.'"[20]

Noah lived for 350 years after the flood, dying at the ripe old age of 950. He died well after the birth of Abraham, although the two most likely did not meet.

Noah is mentioned several times in the New Testament and praised in Hebrews as a hero of faith: "It was faith that made Noah hear God's warnings about things in the future that he could not see. He obeyed God and built a boat in which he and his family were saved. As a result, the world was condemned, and Noah received from God the righteousness that comes by faith."[21]

DID NOAH REALLY LIVE 950 YEARS?

The Bible says Noah was 600 years old when the Flood came and then he lived 350 years more—950 years total. Is that for real?

Such a long life was not unusual before the Flood. The Bible says the ages of the first patriarchs at their deaths were—Adam was 930; Seth was 912; Enosh was 905; Cainan was 910; Mahalalel was 895; Jared was 962; Methuselah was 969; Lamech was 777; and Noah was 950.

If you think the ages given in the Bible is a long time, the first eight kings in the ancient Sumerian king list all reigned between 18,600 years and 43,200 years.

After the Flood, the ages of the patriarchs at their deaths, according to the Bible, decreased from Shem (one of Noah's sons) at 600 years to Terah at 205 years and his son, Abraham, at 175 years. That's still rather old, but it's young compared to Noah's 950 years.

An interesting thing is that after the eighth Sumerian king, who reigned 18,600 years, Sumerian history says a great flood swept over the land and then came the First Dynasty of Kish, in which, according to the Sumerian king list, the kings reigned from 1,500 years to 140 years—decidedly less than 43,200 years.

How do we explain these extremely large numbers? It should be no surprise there is no agreed-upon explanation. But three possibilities are:

- **mathematical**—you have to divide the Sumerian numbers by 3,600 (the explanation for this includes a possible scribal error and the Sumerian use of a base 60 numeral system) and the Bible numbers by 12 (because, this explanation says, the Bible is actually talking about months).
- **literal**—the patriarchs really did live long lives and the Flood caused environmental and genetic changes that have shortened our lives.
- **symbolic**—the large numbers are a way of ascribing honor to the ancient patriarchs.

2.
FLOOD STORIES AROUND THE WORLD

Ashurbanipal, the last great king of the ancient Assyrian empire, was a mighty leader who defeated Egypt and Babylon. He was popular with his subjects and brutal to his enemies. His most memorable accomplishment, though, was the creation of an unparalleled Royal Library containing twenty thousand to thirty thousand tablets. Astrological studies, dictionaries, literature, scientific texts, and religious writings were all included in this organized repository of Assyrian knowledge.

In 1851, British archaeologist Henry Layard discovered Ashurbanipal's Royal Library in Ninevah (in modern Iraq, and, yes, it's the same Ninevah where God sent Jonah to preach after he got out of the belly of the great fish). Layard boxed up thousands of tablets and shipped them to the British Museum in London, where they sat for twenty years.

Thirty-two-year-old George Smith had "an amazing ability to look at a piece of clay that to everyone else looked like a dog biscuit and know what the words meant."[22] One fall morning in 1872, as Smith examined some tablets from Ashurbanipal's Royal Library that he had carefully pieced together, "My eye caught the statement that the ship rested on the mountains of Nizir," he said, "followed by the account of sending forth the dove, and its finding no resting place and returning."

George Smith was the first person in thousands of years to read the Epic of Gilgamesh, one of the oldest surviving works of literature that had been buried in Ashurbanipal's library. Smith was stunned by the similarity between the eleventh tablet and the story of Noah.

The Epic tells the story of Gilgamesh, the king of Uruk (the actual city of Uruk has been excavated) who was oppressing his people. The gods created from clay a primitive man, Enkidu, who was incensed at Gilgamesh's mistreatment of Uruk's citizens and fought him. However, Gilgamesh and Enkidu became friends and eventually Enkidu died. As Gilgamesh grieved his friend's death, he realized he, too, could die and decided to learn the secret of eternal life from Utnapishtim, one of the survivors of the great flood. After many perilous adventures, Gilgamesh reached the island where Utnapishtim lived. Here's where the story gets interesting.

Utnapishtim told Gilgamesh that the god Ea had told him (Utnapishtim) to build a boat to save himself from a great flood. It was to be a square—120 cubits per side—have six decks, divided into compartments, and covered with bitumen and pitch. Utnapsihtim went into the boat with his family, his silver and gold, the people who helped him build the boat, and "all the animals of the field." Then came such a terrible six-day storm that the gods themselves were frightened and "wailed like a woman in labor" and the land was flattened. All humans not in the boat were turned to clay.

Utnapishtim sent out a dove and then a swallow, both of which came back to him, and then a raven, which was able to find food and so did not come back. This let Utnaphishtim know he could let the people and animals out of the boat. He then sacrificed a sheep, and the chief god, Enlil, granted Utnapishtim and his wife eternal life, which was the point of Utnapishtim's telling the story to Gilgamesh.

When George Smith described the Epic of Gilgamesh to a "large and distinguished company assembled in the rooms of the Society of Biblical Archaeology" the audience was astounded at the similarity of the flood story in the epic poem with the story told in Genesis.

The story of Noah and the ark is not unique. More than three hundred stories of great floods are found around the world from South America to India to Australia.

The oldest known flood story is on a tablet from the seventeenth century BC, hundreds of years before Genesis was written, and one of several similar flood stories from Sumeria (Iraq), one of the world's earliest civilizations. Mankind's excessive noise was keeping the chief god awake, so the gods decided to destroy all human beings with a flood. Enki (one of the gods) warned Ziusudra, ruler of Shuruppak and a man known for his humility and obedience, to build a large boat. After a seven-day storm in which "the huge boat is tossed about on the great waters," Ziusudra opened a window and offered a sacrifice of an ox and a sheep. When the flood was over, the animals left the boat.

The stories of Utnapishtim and Ziusudra and Noah have many similarities and all come from the same part of the world. Other stories, however, have less in common, but there are still remarkably common elements. Here are four of those.

HINDU

According to a sacred Hindu text,[23] Manu, the first king to rule the earth, was washing his hands in a river when a tiny fish asked Manu to protect him from larger fish. "You will be rewarded for your kindness," the fish said. Manu took pity on the fish and placed him in a large bowl. When the fish outgrew the bowl, Manu put him in a pool, and then in larger and larger bodies of water as the fish grew until Manu finally put the fish in the ocean.

The fish revealed to Manu that he was actually an avatar of Vishnu, a supreme god, and warned Manu, "who was endued with great wisdom and devoted to virtue," of a coming flood that would destroy all the people on the earth. The fish told him to build a boat with a strong rope on its prow and to take seven enlightened people (Rishi), seeds from every kind of plant, and animals to repopulate the earth.

When the flood came, Manu tied the rope onto a horn growing out of the fish and the fish pulled the boat to the top of a high mountain protruding from the flood waters. The boat remained there until the waters receded. Manu then performed a sacrifice, pouring butter and sour milk onto the waters. After a year, a woman was born from the waters, and from Manu and the woman came a new human race that replenished the earth.

Manu and the seven rishis (enlightened people) are saved from the great flood by Matsya, the avatar in the form of a fish of the Hindu god Vishnu. The boat's rope is tied to a horn growing out of the fish. (Wikipedia)

GREEK

Prometheus was one of the Greek Titans, the earliest gods in the Greek pantheon. Titans had incredible strength, but were later overthrown by younger gods, the Olympians. Prometheus was given the task of creating humankind from clay, but although Zeus wanted to keep humans from having fire, Prometheus stole it from heaven and gave it to them. In punishment for his rebellious act, Prometheus was chained to a rock on top of a mountain where every day an eagle would feed on his liver. During the night his liver would grow back, only to be eaten again the next day.

After Prometheus was bound to the rock, Zeus sent disease and worry into the world and humans became more and more wicked, violent, and lawless. Eventually Zeus said, "These men are nothing but a source of trouble" and decided to destroy them with water.

Living in Thessaly, a region in ancient Greece, was Deucalion, son of Prometheus. He was a common man—not a Titan like his father—and was known for his good deeds, piety, and uprightness. Once a year he would visit his father, who knew the future and warned Deucalion that Zeus would destroy the earth with a flood. Deucalion built a boat and gathered food and supplies. When the rains started, Deucalion and his wife, Pyrrha, boarded the boat and safely rode out the rising waters, knowing that all other people would be drowned.

As the waters began to recede, the boat landed on Mount Parnassus. Trees, flowers, and grasses survived the flood, but Deucalion and Pyrrha were the only humans left. As they started to walk down the mountain, they encountered a tall noble-looking man who was Hermes, messenger of the gods. They told Hermes of their desire to see the earth populated again. He said they should "throw the bones of your great mother over your shoulder." They understood their "mother" to be the earth and "bones" to be stones. So they threw stones over their shoulders.

The stones Deucalion threw became full-grown men, strong, handsome, and brave, and the stones Pyrrha threw became full-grown women, lovely and fair. Deucalion became their king, and he and Pyrrha had a son, Hellen. They named the country Hellas, after their son, and the people were called the Hellenes—another name for people who live in Greece.

There are several variations of the story of Deucalion and Pyrrha, but the most complete one was told by the Roman poet Ovid in his *Metamorphoses*, written about the time of Christ. Later versions of the story add details that sound as if they were adapted from the biblical story of Noah. For instance in the first century AD, Plutarch says Deucalion sent out pigeons to see if the land was dry, and in a second-century AD version, Deucalion took pairs of animals with him on the boat. It is possible Plutarch knew of the story of Noah in Genesis.

OJIBWE / CHIPPEWA

The Anishinaabe Nation, called Ojibwe in Canada and Chippewa in the United States, live around the Great Lakes. The Ottawa, which have a similar story, are related to the Anishinaabe, but are a distinct people. Long ago the Anishinaabe people began to argue and fight. The Great Spirit, or Gitchi-Manitou, decided to purify the earth with a flood that would destroy the Anishinaabe people and most of the animals.

When the flood came, only Nanabozho—an important figure in many Anishinaabe stories; he even has his own Facebook

Nanabozho, a spirit in Anishinaabe stories who appears
in various forms, waits in a tree during the flood before
floating on a log with some animals. This picture is from
R.C. Armour's book *North American Indian Fairy Tales
Lolklore and Legends*, 1905. (Wikipedia)

page—survived by floating on a huge log with a few animals. (The Ottawa version says he was in a great canoe with many pairs of animals and birds, rowed by a most beautiful maiden.) "I am going to swim to the bottom of this water and grab a handful of earth," he said. "With this small bit of earth, I believe we can create a new land for us to live on with the help of the Four Winds and Gitchi-Manitou."

But Nanabozho was not able to reach the bottom. The loon, the grebe, the mink, and other animals also tried to reach the bottom, but failed. Then the muskrat said he would try. The other animals laughed and made fun of the muskrat. "Only Gitchi-Manitou can place judgment on others," said Nanabozho. "If muskrat wants to try, he should be allowed to." After a very long time, the muskrat floated to the surface. He had died, but in his paw was a small ball of earth. The muskrat had given his life so life on earth could start again after the flood.

The turtle then offered to "use my back to bear the weight of this piece of earth." The little ball of earth the muskrat had brought up grew and grew on the turtle's back, becoming an island today known as North America. The Ottawa version says the maiden and Nanabozho repopulated the world.

MAASAI

A flood story with much similarity to the biblical account comes from the Maasai, a semi-nomadic people who live in Kenya and northern Tanzania. Tumbainot was a righteous man whose wife, Naipande, bore him three sons. When his brother died, Tumbainot married his brother's wife also. (A common custom in many cultures, a man's marrying his brother's widow is called a levirate marriage in the Bible and *ukungenwa* in South Africa.) She bore Tumbainot three more sons.

People were sinful, but there had not been a murder. When a man named Nambija killed another man, God decided to destroy all mankind except Tumbainot and his family. At God's command, Tumbainot built a large boat of wood and took on the boat his two wives, six sons and their wives, animals of every sort, and provisions.

God sent rain, which drowned all living things except those on the boat. When his provisions got low, Tambainot released a dove that returned to him because the floodwaters were still high. A few days later he released a vulture after attaching an arrow to one of its tail feathers. If the vulture returned without the arrow, Tumbainot thought, it would be because it had hooked on to something, indicating that the water was receding. That evening the vulture returned without the arrow. The boat came to rest in a prairie, and when Tambainot got off, he saw four rainbows, which, he believed, was a sign the wrath of God was over.

Most cultures have a flood story as part of their mythology. Dr. John Morris analyzed more than two hundred such stories and said if the common features are combined, the story would read something like this: (the percentages are the percentage of the stories he analyzed containing the element, for instance 88 percent of the stories involve one righteous family)

FLOOD STORIES AROUND THE WORLD

Once there was a worldwide (95 percent) flood, sent by god to judge the wickedness of man (66 percent). But one righteous family (88 percent) was forewarned (66 percent) of the coming flood. They built a boat (70 percent) on which they survived the flood along with the animals (67 percent). As the flood ended, their boat landed on a high mountain (57 percent) from which they descended and repopulated the whole earth. [24]

Interestingly, nine percent of the stories say specifically that eight people were saved and seven percent mention a rainbow.

Why are there so many flood stories with so many comment elements? Perhaps some accounts borrow details from other stories. This is the reason given for the similarities in Middle Eastern flood stories such as the Gilgamesh Epic, the Sumerian story of Ziusudra, and the Genesis account of Noah.

Perhaps floods are a common disaster and people tell stories about them. For instance, some stories are connected with an unusual flooding of the Euphrates River (See page 36) or a filling of the Persian Gulf after the last Ice Age. Others are connected with a Mediterranean tsunami caused by a volcanic eruption on the Greek island of Thera, just north of Crete, in about 1600 BC—one of the largest eruptions in recorded history. North American stories are connected with the draining at the end of the last Ice Age of Lake Agassiz, an immense lake larger than all the Great Lakes combined that covered much of Manitoba, eastern Saskatchewan and North Dakota, and northern Minnesota. Still other stories are said to have originated with the flooding of the Black Sea (See page 39) or a six-hundred-foot-high tsunami caused by a meteor crashing into the Indian Ocean in 2800 to 3000 BC.

Or perhaps these stories from around the world are a collective memory of an actual Great Flood that covered the entire earth.

DID ANCIENT CHINESE KNOW ABOUT THE FLOOD?

While there are only twenty-six letters in the English language, there are tens of thousands of Chinese characters, although a person needs to know fewer than four thousand to be functionally literate. The earliest Chinese characters were probably mostly pictograms—where the character looks like the thing it represents—and ideograms, although they have evolved to where they are hard to recognize.

Sun

Mountain

Horse

Today only about four percent of Chinese characters are pictograms, but one is particularly intriguing—the character for "ship" or "large boat." It's formed by combining the words for "boat," "eight" (the number of people on the ark), and "person."

Large Ship   **Eight**   **Person**   **Boat**

A delightful illustration from a fifteenth-century Flemish manuscript is more interested in telling the story of the Flood than picturing a sea-worthy boat.

3.
WATER, WATER EVERYWHERE

"On that day all the fountains of the great deep burst forth, and the windows of the heavens were opened. And rain fell upon the earth forty days and forty nights.... The flood continued forty days on the earth.... And the waters prevailed so mightily on the earth that all the high mountains under the whole heaven were covered. The waters prevailed above the mountains, covering them fifteen cubits deep." (Genesis 7:11-12, 17, 19-20)

Was the entire earth covered in water as the Bible says? Most students of the Bible thought the Flood was a global one until about 250 years ago when major problems began to be discussed. For instance, there's not enough water on earth to cover Everest, Kilimanjaro, or McKinley. Some people said a wooden boat the size of the biblical ark would not be seaworthy; it would spring hundreds of leaks and sink. Others said even though the ark was huge, it was not large enough to house two of every of tens of thousands species for a year. And those who argue for a local flood—which can be a really big flood, but not one that covers the entire earth—say there's no discernible evidence for a global flood covering the entire planet. Global flood advocates have answers to these "problems," but to some extent, it's a matter of seeing what you want to see.

Here are three views of the Flood: Noah's Flood told the story of a freak event on the Euphrates River in ancient Sumeria; Noah's Flood told the story of the Mediterranean's flooding the Black Sea; and Noah's Flood actually covered the entire earth.

NOAH'S FLOOD TOLD THE STORY
OF A FREAK EVENT ON THE EUPHRATES RIVER
IN ANCIENT SUMERIA

About five thousand years ago Shuruppak, a Sumerian city about one hundred miles south of modern Baghdad, was a major distribution center for grain, beer, and other goods delivered to towns up and down the Euphrates River—all the way to the powerful city-state of Ur at the southern end. The Euphrates, the longest and one of the most important rivers in Western Asia, begins in eastern Turkey and flows through Syria and Iraq, where it joins the Tigris River. Together they empty into the Persian Gulf.

Ziusudra, one of the city's most successful merchants, was also king of Shuruppak. He would have looked like a Sumerian with heavy eye makeup, a bald head, and even a long kilt.

Ziusudra, a successful merchant, would have used bills
of sale like this one, written in cueiform script of wedge-
shaped marks on a clay tablet. This particular bill of
sale is for a male slave and a building in Shuruppak.
(Marie-Lan Nguyen, Wikipedia)

Sumerians called themselves "the black-headed people."

Ziusudra realized if he could build a bigger barge, he could
make more money from his trading ventures, but he was lim-
ited by technology. It is speculated he built smaller barges as
pontoons, tied them together, and built a larger structure on
top. He did not build his barge for speed, but for stability on
the Euphrates River.

Some sections of the Euphrates were navigable only when the
river was at its peak, and each spring melting snow in the mountains to the north caused the river to rise, spill over its banks,
and create rich, fertile soil for farming. Because he could navigate

the entire river in May or June each year, Ziusudra would fill his large barge with grain, beer, livestock, lumber, textiles, and other cargo, and set off on his trading trips.

Normally when the river was at its height, there was never any rain. However, one June in about 2900 BC, a freak storm came up—perhaps a hurricane or a tropical storm. Ziusudra and his family were banqueting on the barge before he set off with his boatload of goods and animals. The storm was so sudden the barge could not be safely evacuated. The rain lasted between seven days and forty days, and during this time Ziusudra, his wife, his family, and his cargo were at the mercy of the raging Euphrates.

When the rain finally stopped, Ziusudra could not see land for at least seven days. If he had still been on the Euphrates, he would have been able to drink the water, but salty water indicated his family had been swept all the way to the Persian Gulf. The only thing they had to drink was the beer they had on board.

Ziusudra, his family, and his barge landed five hundred miles south of Shurappak on the shores of the Persian Gulf, and they never returned home. Under Sumerian law, even though he was king, Ziusudra would have been sold into slavery if he could not repay his debts. One Babylonian reference suggests Ziusudra and his family settled in Dilmun, the modern island of Bahrain.

This version of the Sumerian flood story was recounted in a 2003 BBC video, *Noah's Ark: The Real Story*. First, critics of a global flood identified what they felt were problems with the Noah story. The video then recounted Ziusudra's story in what it called a "historically accurate picture of the real Noah, where he lived, and what he might have looked like," a statement that assumes the story of Ziusudra and the Gilgamesh Epic were both sources of the Bible's story.

NOAH'S FLOOD TOLD THE STORY OF THE MEDITERRANEAN'S FLOODING THE BLACK SEA

Melting glaciers and rising sea levels is a global concern today. A five-foot rise in the sea level would have a devastating effect on the entire east coast of the U.S. including New York City and Miami. Moreover, a five-foot rise in the sea level would make huge sections of Bangladesh uninhabitable.

If a five-foot rise in the sea level would devastate today's cities, imagine the effect of a *five-hundred-foot* increase! Two scientists say that's what happened to the Black Sea 7,500 years ago:

At first, the rise of the water at the lake's edge was barely noticed.... [But] the new sound was alarming.... The water was muddy. The shore's edge was infested with decaying fish.... The torso of a deer sloshed back and forth in the surf.... Whole trees spun in whirlpools, trunks thrown like splinters into the air, then falling out of sight into waves cresting around boulders. A face of the steep slope collapsed in an avalanche that disappeared into the water, completely flushed away.... The blast of a torrent beat on the witnesses, overwhelming their senses. Petrified by the joining of the ocean and the lake, they staggered back from the precipice and fled homeward to tell of the chaos unleashed by the gods and the doom it foretold.[25]

The Black Sea, north of Turkey and south of Russia and Ukraine, is five times the size of Lake Superior, America's largest lake. It is connected to the Aegean Sea and the Mediterranean by the Bosphorus Strait that is eighteen miles long and less than two miles wide, the Sea of Marmara, and the Dardanelles that is thirty-eight miles long and less than four miles wide. The two straits and Marmara make up the Turkish Straits. Today the Bosphorus Strait runs through Istanbul and marks the boundary between Europe and Asia.

Understanding this geography is important in order to realize the effect of one thousand years of especially arid conditions. Without adequate rain, the level of the Black Sea plummeted, cutting it off from the Aegean and Mediterranean Seas by a high piece of land where the Bosphorus Strait is today. The river-fed fresh water of the Black Sea made its shoreline especially fertile and people settled along what was one of the world's largest fresh-water lakes and developed an early farming culture.

When the last Ice Age ended, water released from vast ice sheets returned to the ocean, causing sea levels to rise. In about 5600 BC, salt water from the rising Mediterranean and Aegean began to spill into the Black Sea through the Turkish Straits, eventually at a rate two hundred times the flow over Niagara Falls. At its most devastating, the level of the Black Sea rose a foot a day, submerging in some places about a half mile of land. The flooding lasted for at least one hundred days until sixty thousand square miles were inundated, increasing the size of the Sea by 30 percent. Those living around the Black Sea fled for their lives.

The Turkish Straits connects the Black Sea with
the Aegean Sea.

In 1999, marine geologists William Ryan and Walter Pitman
from Columbia University explained their proposed history of
the flooding of the Black Sea in their best-selling book, *Noah's
Flood: The New Scientific Discoveries about the Event that Changed
History* and speculated that farmers fled the encroaching waters
and went to Europe where they took their farming skills. They
also asked if the tremendous year-long flood became part of folk
memory and inspired the stories later retold in the Babylonian
Gilgamesh Epic and the biblical story of Noah.

"Creationists were outraged," said David Montgomery. "This
flood was not an earth-shattering, topography-busting flood that
ripped apart and reassembled the whole world.... They saw the
suggestion that Noah's Flood was a regional disaster, and not a
global event, as an attack on Christianity. For completely different reasons, many geologists also were immediately skeptical—
hadn't science dispelled Noah's Flood as an ancient myth?"[26] But
the story of the Black Sea flood doesn't end there.

Robert Ballard, one of the world's most famous underwater explorers—he discovered the *Titanic* and the German battleship *Bismarck*—was fascinated with the story Ryan and Pitman told and decided to look for evidence. Using advanced robotic technology, he found an ancient shoreline submerged four hundred feet under the current surface of the Black Sea. He started mapping it and discovered tools, ceramics, freshwater mollusk remains, and evidence of houses. In 2012, his team discovered "one very large shipwreck our last week there," and in December, 2012, he told ABC News, "I'm convinced that we will find evidence of a civilization from the time of Noah at the bottom of the Black Sea. We're going back next summer to look."

NOAH'S FLOOD ACTUALLY COVERED THE ENTIRE EARTH

Dr. John Morris has a PhD in Geological Engineering and is president of the Institute for Creation Research. He explained why he believes the waters of the Flood covered the entire earth in his book The Global Flood.[27]

Until the late 1700s, most people who read the Bible took at face value what Genesis said: "all the high mountains were covered" with water. However, when explorers reported finding lofty mountains such as the Himalayas, a flood with enough water to cover them seemed implausible and many adopted the view that the Great Flood was local. Their conclusions assumed the world before the Flood was like the world today. But it wasn't. The tallest mountains we know today did not exist in their present form before the Flood.

Uniformitarianism is the assumption that the processes operating in the world now always operated in the same way. It's an assumption that dominates education today, especially those sciences dealing with the past. There's a certain comfort in assuming that processes have always operated as they do now because it allows conclusions to be derived from observations. But if the assumption of uniformity of processes is wrong, the conclusions will be wrong.

A more realistic approach is catastrophism, which says the earth was formed by sudden violent events. Uniformitarianism requires extremely long periods of time to explain the changes we see in the earth. Catastrophism allows for more rapid changes in the earth. The eruption of Mount St. Helens in 1980, which blew off the entire top of the mountain, is a good example of a local catastrophic event. The Great Flood is the best example of a global catastrophic event.

At the time of the Flood, there was most likely one supercontinent, sometimes called Pangea. This land mass was relatively flat and surrounded by a single global ocean. When God decided to destroy humans because of their wickedness and also animals, a supernatural, cataclysmic, and global series of events occurred that caused the Flood.

First, "All the fountains of the great deep burst forth"—perhaps underwater volcanoes all erupting at the same time, sending huge volumes of sub-surface fluids onto the land. Imagine the tsunamis and devastation that would cause!

Second, "The windows of the heavens were opened"—we don't know what this was, but it was different from normal rain and undoubtedly more intense.

Third, "Rain fell upon the earth forty days and forty nights."

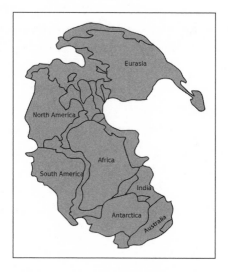

When Pangaea, a supercontinent, broke apart, the modern continents that are outlined here moved into their current positions. (Wikipedia)

Water from all these sources covered Pangea entirely. And the same tectonic forces contributing to the Flood caused Pangea to begin to break apart. What is usually called "continental drift" was more like a "continental sprint" as the continents moved into the positions we know today. The Himalayan Mountains were formed when India slammed into Asia. The Rocky Mountains were formed when two plates came together. The time of the Flood was a violent time. Continents were rising and spreading apart as ocean basins sank, giving rise to immense fractures in the earth's crust. Shock waves repeatedly reverberated throughout the ocean, bringing unimaginable devastation to sea life. Waves of water and loose sediments carrying sea creatures were pushed inland. Storms dozens of times greater than present hurricanes buffeted the earth.

After months of turmoil, the waters drained into newly deepened and widened ocean basins, exposing dry land. The tectonic movement of continents facilitated the water draining into the oceans. Also, "God made a wind blow over the earth," and this pushed the water into the deepening ocean basins and helped evaporate water from the soggy ground. Gradually, the land became dry and the water table lowered.

The Flood's destabilization of climate patterns, ocean temperatures, and ocean currents contributed to the last great Ice Age. Volcanic aerosols thrown into the atmosphere during the Flood would have shielded the earth from much of the solar radiation we now receive, thereby cooling the continents and allowing snow to form into great ice sheets. It was a period of residual catastrophism in which catastrophes operated on a smaller scale than the Great Flood, but they still devastated entire regions of the earth.

When Noah, his family, and the animals left the ark, they encountered an unfamiliar world. The geography had changed. Plant and animal life had been devastated. Weather patterns were chaotic. The jet streams, the ocean currents, and the continental movements had not yet stabilized. God's reassurance to Noah was significant: "Never again shall there be a flood to destroy the earth." And God's sign of that promise—a rainbow—was universal.

Was the Flood a worldwide flood or a local flood? The Bible indicates it was global in extent and dynamic in nature. And God's promise is that a flood will not happen again. If the Flood in Noah's day were a local flood, God would have broken His promise in 1931 in China, in 1949 in Guatemala, and in 1974 in Bangladesh. The China flood killed nearly three million people, and the Guatemala and Bangladesh floods killed tens of thousands each.

It's tempting to say, "Here are three scenarios. Decide for yourself which is true." But your deciding which scenario you think is true usually has more to do with your presuppositions than anything else. And your decision probably has very little to do with which scenario actually is true because truth is discovered by inquiry, not elected by a majority vote.

David Montgomery says, "the rocks don't lie" (it's the title of his book). John Morris says, "the Bible doesn't lie." And both men would probably agree with the statement of the other. However, David Montgomery and John Morris differ on what the rocks are telling us. And they differ on what the Bible is telling us.

The problem comes when we turn the statements around and say, "the rocks *do* lie" or "the Bible *does not* tell the truth." Then we make assumptions that keep us from seeing the truth. David Montgomery tells a fascinating story to illustrate this.

"It is hard to see evidence for what you're sure cannot exist," he said. "Twentieth-century geologists were no exception to this rule. They were certain that enormous floods capable of sculpting topography were impossible. Until, that is… J. Harlen Bretz uncovered evidence of giant floods in eastern Washington in the 1920s [and] it took most of the twentieth century for other geologists to believe him. Geologists had so thoroughly denied the existence of great floods that they could not believe it when somebody actually found evidence for one."[28]

Listen carefully to what the Bible has to say. And listen carefully to what the rocks have to say. And don't rule out the truth in either.

The Nuremberg Chronicle (named after the German city in which it was published), one of the first printed books to successfully integrate illustrations and text, was published in Latin fewer than 50 years after Gutenberg invented movable type. It is a combination biblical paraphrase and world history. Here Noah and his family and some helpers build the ark. Notice the top of the boat says, "Archa Noe"—Noah's ark. (Wikipedia)

4.
HOW BIG WAS THE ARK?

God told Noah, "The length of the ark shall be three hundred cubits, its width fifty cubits, and its height thirty cubits.... You shall make it with lower, second, and third decks." "What's a cubit?" Noah asked God, according to Bill Cosby. "Let's see," said God. "I used to know what a cubit was...."

In the ancient world the cubit was the most common unit of measure—the length of a man's forearm from his elbow to the tip of his middle finger. Usually considered to be eighteen inches, the cubit was divided into six "palms," each with four "fingers"—twenty-four fingers to a cubit.

At 18 inches per cubit, the ark would be 450 feet long, 75 feet wide (1½ times the length and half the width of a football field) and 45 feet high—one of the largest wooden boats ever built. You can be pretty sure the ark did not look like what most of us remember from a nursery picture or from a storybook—a cute boat with a deck full of animals. It was shaped like a long box, not like a seagoing vessel built for speed. In fact, some scholars think the word for "ark" may be related to the Egyptian word for "coffin."

The word *ark* is itself confusing. The English Bible uses *ark* as a name for both Noah's boat and for the holy box containing the Ten Commandments, Aaron's rod, a jar of manna, and the Torah scroll written by Moses—the ark made famous by Indiana Jones in *Raiders of the Lost Ark*. But Hebrew uses two very different words for these two objects—and uses *tebah* only for Noah's ark and for the basket in which baby Moses was placed by his mother. We don't know if *tebah* means a boat, something covered in pitch, a certain shape, something that preserves life—or something else.

According to the Bible, Noah's ark had three decks with rooms (which would provide structural support), a door, and a window. Some point out there was probably not just one window, but a row of them just under the roof. Georgie Hagopian, who claimed to have seen the ark in the early 1900s, said the roof was nearly flat except for a row of windows, fifty or more, estimated to be eighteen inches by thirty inches, running from front to back covered by an overhanging roof.

The ark was made of gopherwood—whatever that is. Translators had no idea what the Hebrew word *gopher* meant and so they merely transliterated it. When you say "gopher," you're saying a Hebrew word with an unknown meaning. The oldest Greek translation calls gopherwood "squared timber." The most popular Latin translation calls it "smoothed wood." Some have thought it is cedar or cypress. But the bottom line is…we don't know.

God said to cover the ark inside and outside with "pitch," probably for waterproofing, although there is no agreement on whether the pitch was an oil-based substance (as it is thought of today) or a gum-based resin extracted from trees, or something else.

Although the Bible says God gave certain specifications for the ark, it was Noah who had to design it—how to house the animals, where to build the living quarters for his family, what design elements would make the ark the most seaworthy. There is much speculation on how he did it—primarily by those who want to demonstrate it is possible.

For instance, Tim Lovett, an Australian mechanical engineer who has extensively studied the ark, says a long ship like the ark could ride out waves comfortably if it were to ride across the waves. But if it rode the waves sideways, the boat would roll dangerously and might even capsize. Lovett suggests the ark may have had a projection on the front to catch the wind and a skeg or fixed rudder at the rear. The two would cause the ark to act like a weather vane, turning it into the wind with the result that it would ride across the waves.

Another problem for which Lovett suggests a solution is the seaworthiness of a wooden boat as big as the ark. Admittedly it did not have to go anywhere—so speed was not important—but Australian nautical archaeologist Tom Vosmer says not even nineteenth century boat builders could have built a wooden boat that size. "It's a safe bet that the huge ark would spring hundreds of leaks along the length of its huge hull and sink like a stone."[29] Vosmer is correct in that large wooden ships such as the *HMS Orlando* (nineteenth century, 336 feet long) and the *Wyoming* (twentieth century, 330 feet long) were said to flex with waves to such an extent as to be noticeable. Lovett explains such flexing would cause the wood planks to slide against each other, breaking the waterproofing seal. But perhaps earlier boat builders had a different approach.

Ancient shipbuilders—both Greeks at least four centuries before Christ and Egyptians around 2,500 BC—used a labor-intensive approach to hull construction Lovett calls edge-jointed planking, a form of mortise and tenon joints similar to biscuit joints used by woodworkers. Noah also could have used more than one layer of planking and held everything together with wooden pegs, which have the advantage of expanding and tightening when they get wet. And, of course, the boat was covered with pitch inside and out.

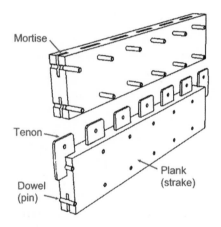

Edge-jointed planking is a labor-intensive way of building ship hulls in which a tenon is inserted into a mortise hole formed in the edge of a plank. The tenon could then be secured by a dowel. This method gives greater strength to the hull than a ship that relies on the strength of the frame. (Tim Lovett)

It's possible the ark could have had one or more "moon pools," openings in the bottom of the ship with sides extending inside the ship well above the waterline. From the inside, the moon pool would look like a swimming pool in the floor of the ark. Water would not come into the ark because of the moon pool's sides. Today, moon pools are used in drilling ships to give technicians access below the ship and in ships that support professional divers to give them access to the water. Moon pools in the ark could serve two purposes: (1) a place to dispose of animal refuse, and (2) as a means of creating some air circulation as water rose and fell in the pool.

In the Ming Dynasty, Chinese treasure ships were reported to be the same length as the ark and twice as wide. They were the most technically advanced vessels in the world and in the early 1400s they traveled to India, Africa, and perhaps even Australia. We don't know if they flexed, but they were seaworthy. However, some people question the validity of their reported size "on practical engineering grounds"[30] just as Vosmer questions the size of the ark because he says it would spring hundreds of leaks.

The ark has fascinated people for centuries and has been one of the favorite subjects for artists. The Morgan Crusader Bible, one of the most beautiful medieval illustrated Bibles, was commissioned by Louis IX of France in 1240. It includes a picture of a house with Noah and his family in it on top of a U-shaped boat, which held the animals. A fifteenth century Flemish manuscript contains a delightful picture of an ark full of animals. (See page 34.)

In 1493, a history of the world, called *The Nuremberg Chronicle*, pictured Noah and his sons and workers building

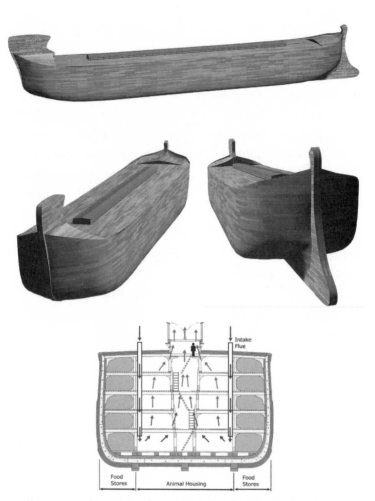

Three views of a model of the ark made by ark researcher Tim Lovett show its amazing length, a projection on the front to catch the wind, and a fixed rudder at the rear. Lovett also proposes several ways in which ventilation could have been achieved. The one pictured here has flue pipes that allow fresh air to enter the ark from the top and then as it is warmed by animal heat rise to the top through the animal cages. Lovett suggests that food could have been stored along the outside hull wall. (Tim Lovett)

an ark with a hull that looked similar to the ships used by Christopher Columbus. (See page 48.)

In the early 1600s, according to a book published in 1728, a Dutch merchant studied the Noah story and built a ship in the same proportions as the ark, but at one-quarter scale—120 feet long. At first people made fun of him, but his boat behaved steadily on the ocean because of less wind and water resistance and it held about 30 percent more cargo with the same number of sailors as other ships.

One of the more intriguing pictures of the ark was made in 1985 by California artist and ark researcher Elfred Lee. In 1915, the Ottoman government (today's Turkey) began a massacre that killed more than one million Armenians. One who escaped the genocide was Georgie Hagopian, who grew up near Ararat and said his uncle, a devout man, took him to the ark twice, in 1908 and 1910. When Georgie returned home, he discovered many of his young friends had also been shown the ark. Evidently it was a rather common Armenian pilgrimage.

The ark, Georgie said, was very long and rectangular with more than 50 windows just under an overhanging roof. The wood was so hard that when his uncle shot his musket at the ark, the pellets just dropped, hardly making a dent. The ark was covered with green moss.

Georgie didn't know anyone cared about his story until 1970 when he was encouraged to tell it to a group interested in finding the ark. He described the details of what he remembered to Elfred Lee, who drew a picture of what Georgie saw. Georgie died in 1972. (See page 60.)

INTERVIEW WITH PATRICK MARSH

Patrick Marsh has one of the world's most fun jobs. He's worked on the 1984 Olympic Games in Los Angeles, helped design the Statue of Liberty celebration, and was the Set Designer for the King Kong and Jaws attractions at Universal Studios theme park in Florida. Now he's in charge of the design of a 510-foot life-sized replica of the ark being built as the central attraction of the Ark Encounter theme park in Willamstown, Kentucky, just south of Cincinnati.

The mental picture most of us have of the ark is based on a bathtub toy with a pair of giraffes sticking their heads out the top. It's no wonder that with this impression, we think the story of Noah in the Bible is an impossible fable. It's hard to get your mind wrapped around what the ark was really like. However, if you can see it—the immense size of the ark, its proportion, its interior, how it was built—you can understand how the story of Noah in the Bible is not only possible, but makes sense.

By being immersed in both the historical and biblical world of Noah and by walking through the replica we are building, visitors to Ark Encounter will see how Noah and his family lived on the ark and how they took care of the animals. The ark will be part of a theme park, which will also have an ancient walled city, the Tower of Babel, The Ten Plagues of Egypt ride, a First Century Village, and more.

The ark itself will be as close to Noah's ark as we can determine. It will be 510 feet long instead of 450 feet because we used the Nippur Cubit, which is longer than twenty inches. Inside will be three levels, pens for the animals, facilities for feeding them, and living quarters for Noah and his family. We'll have live animals—the smaller ones—and both static and animatronic animals. We don't have to make our ark seaworthy because we're not expecting a flood.

Most people want to know how Noah could have fit all the animals on the ark because they usually assume he had to take two of every species—and there are more than a million non-insect species. However, we have a research group led by Georgia Purdom, who has a doctorate in molecular genetics from Ohio State University, that has determined only a few thousand pairs of animals, plus seven of what the Bible calls "clean animals," would have to be brought on the ark. Noah did not have to bring two terriers and two pit bulls onto the ark, just two dogs. At the most, there were two thousand pairs of families of animals. This includes horses and elephants and dinosaurs, but the smaller animals were more numerous. With three decks running the length of the 510-foot boat, that's plenty of room for the animals and their food. We'll explain how Noah might have dealt with the challenges of food, water, ventilation, and waste removal for the animals.

People also want to know how Noah and his sons could have built the ark. There's nothing in the Bible to suggest they built it by themselves. Noah could have hired help. It probably took him sixty to seventy-five years. The size of the ark is another challenge, but ancient people were as enamored with huge projects as we are today. For instance, a 455-ton obelisk was set up in ancient Egypt, and then moved to Rome! Given the amount of time he had and that he could have enlisted help, it's reasonable to assume Noah could have built the ark.

We will talk about how Noah and his family lived on the ark, including such basic issues as light (oil lamps were probably

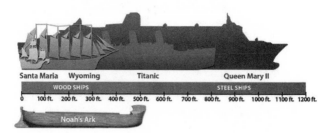

The ark is one of the world's largest wooden ships. Shown here at 510 feet long, it dwarfs the *Santa Maria*, Christopher Columbus's ship, and is even bigger than the *Wyoming*, which was 450 feet long, from tip to tip. Larger ships such as the *Titanic* (882 feet) and *Queen Mary II* (1,132 feet) are made of steel. (courtesy of Answers in Genesis and used by permission)

used), food storage (pottery jars), and cooking (ceramic ovens).

We have two major challenges in building a replica of the ark. First, we don't know much about Noah's world—the society in which he lived before the Flood—and so there is a lot we have to infer from the little we know. We know some people raised livestock, some worked in metal, some were musicians, and they lived long lives. We know there were mighty men and beautiful daughters and that wickedness was great and the earth was corrupt and filled with violence. Beyond that we have reason to believe those who lived before the Flood had advanced technology for architecture and construction, advanced understanding of astronomy, and the ability to travel and build boats. And if life-experience contributes to a person's understanding, just think how much understanding a five-hundred-year-old Noah must have had!

The second challenge is that the Bible tells us only the ark's size and a little about its interior and exterior. It doesn't give us much information. But by studying ancient civilizations and by using logic the way Noah could have, we can draw a lot of conclusions. For instance, today we know how to automatically provide food and water for a dog or cat. Noah undoubtedly used something similar—we'll have examples—so he or his family would have had to refill the container only every two weeks.

But the exhibits won't end with the Flood. In addition to an inspiring diorama that will explain the rainbow as a sign of God's promise to Noah that the earth would never again be destroyed by a flood, we will have an exhibit that will talk about the world after the Flood—the Ice Age, the migration of people and animals, the Tower of Babel, and the dispersion of people into families and language groups. The Ark Encounter theme park is meant to be both entertaining and educational.

Elfred Lee made this picture of the ark from extensive interviews with Georgie Hapopian, who said his uncle had twice taken him to Mount Ararat to see the ark, which seemed to him to be at "the top of the world." The picture shows the uncle lifting the young boy Georgie to a ladder, which may have been added by later pilgrims, so that he could climb to the top of the ark. (courtesy of Elfred Lee and used by permission)

5.
THE ANIMALS WENT IN TWO BY TWO

*"Do you know which animals got aboard Noah's ark?"
an interviewer asked a child. "Yes, the lucky ones."*[31]

*"Johnny, do you think Noah did a lot of fishing
when he was on the ark?" a Sunday school teacher
asked. "No," said Johnny. "How could he with just
two worms?"*

When most people think of Noah's ark, they think of the animals. That's why there are Noah's Ark Animal Hospitals and Clinics in a dozen states, Noah's Ark Animal Shelters, and a Noah's Ark Welfare Association with pets for adoption.

God told Noah, "take with you seven each of every clean animal, a male and his female; two each of animals that are unclean, a male and his female; also seven each of birds of the air, male and female, to keep the species alive on the face of all the earth."[32]

The Bible is not the only flood story to include animals. In fact, two-thirds of the flood myths say animals were saved.

The Buryat of Eastern Siberia say a man built a boat and took on it a pair of all the animals except the mammoth, which he thought was too large to drown. That's why the bones of mammoths can still be found in Siberia.

The people around the Mamberamo River in Papua, Indonesia, say the rising river caused a flood and only a man, his wife, a pig, a cassowary, a kangaroo, and a pigeon escaped.

A legend told by a people in pre-Colombian Mexico says that God told a man to build a large house and to put animals and food in it. When six months of rain came, the house floated and the animals and those who helped to build it were saved.

The Bible says that because of the wickedness of humans God decided to destroy people and animals. He told Noah to make a floating ark, and representatives of the animal world "shall come in to you to keep them alive." Noah was also to take "every sort of food" on the ark for his family and the animals. When the Flood came, all animals not on the ark died, and after the Flood, "all the animals and all the creatures that move along the ground and all the birds…came out of the ark, one kind after another" "so they can multiply on the earth and be fruitful."[33]

That's all the Bible says about the animals on the ark.

No part of the Noah story invites as much criticism or speculation as the animals. RationalWiki[34] lampoons, "Picture seasick giraffes being tossed around." It also quips, "Making the lions and tigers…eat pellets of grain…while surrounded by nice warm living sides of T-bone steaks and…and *filets mignon* would have been a difficult task."

Real questions abound: (a) Was it possible to transport exotic animals to one location in Noah's time? (b) How did Noah store enough meat for the lions and other carnivores to eat for a year? (c) How did Noah take on board a male and female whiptail lizard—an animal that has no males, only females, which produce embryos without fertilization? (d) How could freshwater fish survive in sea water?

Answers have been suggested: (a) In the first century AD—admittedly not as far back as Noah—Romans brought rhinoceroses, elephants, giraffes, crocodiles, lions, and other animals to the Colosseum. It is said that the Emperor Trajan held more than one hundred contests over the course of four months involving eleven thousand animals and ten thousand gladiators. (b) Meat could have been preserved by drying and giant tortoises could have served as the primary source of fresh meat on the ark. (c) Talking about the whiptail lizard is probably a question that doesn't need an answer. God wanted Noah to take enough animals on the ark to facilitate reproduction. For most animals—but not all—it involved a male and female. (d) Freshwater fish "could survive if they have a chance to acclimatize gradually." Jonathan Sarfati said, "I saw this for myself many years ago at Underwater World in Queensland, Australia. They had a freshwater and saltwater fish in the same tank, and achieved this by gradual adjustments to salinity in both fish until they could cope with the same salinity."[35]

For the most part, the answers are speculation. No one can prove *how* Noah actually did something. They can just show it *was possible* to do something.

Here are nine of the most common questions about the animals on the ark. Most of the answers come from those who believe an ark full of animals were saved from a global flood that destroyed the earth. They have to defend their position and show something is possible. Those who do not believe there was an actual ark full of animals and a global flood just have to ask questions. But many, like RationalWiki, succumb to the temptation to go beyond asking questions and slide into ridicule.

The most detailed study of the ark and its animals is *Noah's Ark: A Feasibility Study* by John Woodmorappe, the pen name for a Chicago public school teacher who has a masters degree in geology. Woodmorappe's work has been widely accepted by those who believe in a literal Noah and the ark.

1. How many animals were on the ark?

A lot, but probably not as many as you might think.

The key here is the meaning of "according to their kinds" when God told Noah to take birds, animals, creeping things "male and female…according to their kinds."

Does "kind" mean species? There are millions of species—somewhere between three and thirty million, a rather large range caused in part because taxonomists (biologists who figure out classifications) don't agree on what a species is. The most common definition of a species is a group of organisms that can interbreed and produce fertile offspring.

Or does "kind" mean genus? A group of similar species is a genus. The Boa genus, for instance, includes several snakes, one of which is the Boa constrictor.

Or does "kind" mean family? A group of similar genera (the plural of genus) is a family. *Canidae* is a family that includes dogs, wolves, foxes, jackals, coyotes, and similar animals. Biological families number in the thousands, not the millions. Did Noah take two dachshunds, two beagles, and two grey wolves? Or did he take a pair of animals representing the *Canidae* family?

Many animals did not need to be on the ark for survival. Sea animals, for instance, could survive a flood. Many of the one million species of insects could probably survive without being on the ark. Interestingly, the Bible says, "Everything on the dry land in whose nostrils was the breath of life died," but insects don't have nostrils or lungs. They get their oxygen through their cell walls.

While God told Noah to take two of every kind of animal into the ark, He clarified his instructions so that the animals should be two of every *unclean* animal and "seven of each kind of *clean* animal" and "seven of each kind of the birds of the heavens." The law God gave to Moses hundreds of years later talked about clean animals, which the Jewish people could eat, and unclean animals, which they could not eat. Although the Mosaic Law had not been given at the time of Noah, it was understood and in force at the time the story of Noah and the ark in Genesis was written. People who study the Bible are equally divided on whether there were seven of each clean animal or seven pairs of each clean animal on the ark. We don't know.

John Woodmorappe says if a "kind" means what we call today a genus, there would have to be just under 16,000 animals (8,000 genera). Others say that a "kind" means a family and so there would be about 2,000 animals (1,000 families). We will talk about 16,000 animals on the Ark because many use that number and even RationalWiki "concedes the point for purpose of expediency."

An interesting footnote is why the differentiation between species and genera was made in the first place. John Wilkins of the University of Melbourne says we have the designation "'species' thanks to Noah's Ark."[36] Before the seventeenth century, the words *species* and *genus* were used interchangeably, but as more kinds of animals were discovered, the question arose of how they could all fit on the Ark. In 1668 Bishop John Wilkins (no relation to the Melbourne scholar) published a book proposing a universal language, but at the beginning of the book he also tried to figure out in great detail what species would fit on the Ark. He did not include a mule, for instance, because, he said, it "is a mungrel production [a hybrid], and not to be rekoned as a different species." John Ray, who worked with Wilkins on his book, developed the first biological notion of species as distinct from genus—thanks to a need to figure out how many animals could fit in the ark.

How many animals were on the ark? There were perhaps as many as sixteen thousand. But there didn't have to be hundreds of thousands. A lot—but not as many as you might think.

2. Were dinosaurs on the ark?

If dinosaurs were around, they would have been on the ark.

Dinosaurs are fascinating because this group of diverse animals includes the largest animals to ever walk the earth. Bones of one dinosaur found in Argentina suggest it was 100 feet long and weighed 100 tons. From a few bones found in Colorado in

66

For the more diftinct clearing up of this, I fhall firft lay down feveral tables of the divers fpecies of beafts that were to be received into the Ark, according to the different kinds of food, wherewith they are ufually nourifhed, conteining both the number appointed for each of them, namely, the clean by fevens, and the unclean by pairs, together with a conjecture (for the greater facility of the calculation) what proportion each of them may bear, either to a Beef, or a Sheep, or a Wolf; and then what kind of room may be allotted to the making of fufficient Stalls for their reception.

Beafts feeding on Hay.				Beafts feeding on Fruits, Roots and Infects.				Carnivorous Beafts		
Number.	**Name.**	**Proportion to Beeves.**	**Bredth of Stalls.**	**Number.**	**Name**	**Proportion to Sheep.**	**Bredth of the Stalls.**	**Name**	**Proportion to Wolves.**	**Bredth of Stalls.**
			feet				feet			feet
2	Horfe	3	20	2	Hog	4		2 Lion	4	10
2	Affe	2	12	2	Baboon	2		2 Beare	4	10
2	Camel	4	20	2	Ape	2		2 Tigre	3	8
2	Elephant	8	36	2	Monky			2 Pard	3	8
7	Bull	7	40	2	Sloth			2 Ounce	2	6
7	Urus	7	40	2	Porcupine			2 Cat		
7	Bifons	7	40	2	Hedghog	7 } 20		2 Civet-cat }	2	6
7	Bonafus	7	40	2	Squirril			2 Ferret		
7	Buffalo	7	40	2	Ginny pig			2 Polecat		
7	Sheep	1 }		2	Ant-bear	2		2 Martin		
7	Stepciceros	1 } 30		2	Armadilla	2		2 Stoat	3	6
7	Broad-tail	1 }		2	Tortoife	2		2 Weefle		
7	Goat	1				—		2 Caftor		
7	Stone-buck	1 } 30				21	20	2 Otter		
7	Shamois	1 }						2 Dog	2	6
7	Antilope	1						2 Wolf	2	6
7	Elke	7	30					2 Fox		
7	Hart	4	30					2 Badger	2	6
7	Buck	3	20					2 Jackall		
7	Rein-deer	3	20					2 Caraguya		
7	Roe	2 } 36								
2	Rhinocerot	8 }								
2	Camelopard	6 } 30								
2	Hare	"								
2	Rabbet } Sheep									
2	Marmotto }									
		92	514						27	72

In this enumeration I do not mention the Mule, becaufe 'tis a mungrel production, and not to be rckoned as a diftinct fpecies. And tho it be moft probable, that the feveral varieties of Beeves, namely that which is ftiled *Urus, Bifons, Bonafus* and *Buffalo,* and thofe other varieties reckoned the 1870s but which are now lost, some scientists say the largest dinosaur, Amphicoelias, was nearly 200 feet long and weighed 135 tons—270,000 pounds! But although the Apatosaurus and the Tyrannosaurus Rex get the good press because of their size, most dinosaurs were relatively small—smaller than a turkey.

Dinosaurs are said to have died out sixty-five million years ago. Noah is said to have lived 4,500 to 7,500 years ago. If you accept both of those dates, dinosaurs were not alive to get on the ark.

However, if one or both of those dates is not accurate and dinosaurs and Noah lived at the same time, it raises interesting questions, the most common being how to get a one-hundred-ton animal on the ark. One answer is a pair of young dinosaurs—not old ones—would have been on the ark. God's purpose in saving the animals was so they could reproduce and populate the earth. Younger animals would have been better suited for that purpose than older ones.

Unlike mammals, which stop growing when they become adults, dinosaurs, like reptiles, keep on growing. In September, 2013, for instance, some Mississippi hunters caught a 13½-foot alligator weighing 727 pounds—a very old alligator. Even huge dinosaurs started life quite small. At five years old, a young Apatosaurus would weigh only a ton and then go through growth spurts, gaining as much as five tons per year until reaching its adult weight of 18 tons. It would then continue to grow, but at a slower rate.

It would be no small task to get a 1- to 2-ton dinosaur on the ark and to feed it, but it's a lot more reasonable than thinking a dinosaur on the ark had to be an 18-ton older Apatosaurus.

If dinosaurs lived at the time of Noah, they would have been on the ark. Geologists say that dinosaurs died out more than sixty million years before humans appeared on the earth. Young earth proponents say dinosaurs and humans co-existed.

3. Could all the animals fit on the ark?
If "all" means sixteen thousand, yes.

After going through some elaborate calculations, John Woodmorappe says sixteen thousand animals would require about 46.8 percent of the floor space of a three-deck ark. He appears to be figuring they would need about forty thousand square feet based on several assumptions.

First, he says, "the ark represents temporary confinement of animals in an emergency situation," more analogous to a modern laboratory or an intensive factory farm than to a zoo, which is a "relatively comfortable confinement of animals on a permanent basis."

Second, he assumes the representatives of animals on the ark were juveniles. For instance, he figured an animal weighing more than 2,200 pounds as an adult would be represented on the ark as a 110-pound juvenile. He may have underestimated the weight of some juveniles because a two-year-old African elephant, the heaviest land mammal other than dinosaurs, weighs about 1,900 pounds and a walrus weighs between 100 and 150 pounds at birth and nurses for more than a year before it is weaned. But fewer than 10 percent of all adult mammals weigh more than fifty pounds, and the heaviest reptile (the crocodile, weighing between 880 and 2,200 pounds), bird (the ostrich, weighing between 140 and 320 pounds), and amphibian (the Chinese giant salamander, weighing between 55 and 66 pounds) all weigh much less than the larger mammals. Very few animals weigh more than 2,200 pounds.

Woodmorappe points out that his calculations do not assume cages for small animals were stacked on top of each other. But they could have been. A large truck carrying cattle has room for as many cows as can fit in four hundred square feet—the size of a typical semi-trailer. A large truck carrying chickens, however, has room for as many chickens as can fit in thirty-two hundred square feet because their cages can be stacked eight high.

In addition to the animals themselves, the ark would have needed storage room for water —which Woodmorappe calculates to be about one million gallons weighing 4,461 tons and taking up about 144,000 cubic feet, which was about 9 percent of the ark's 1.5 million cubic feet. However, it was also possible Noah could have collected rainwater for the first forty days.

Noah was also told to take food for his family and the animals. The bulk of the food would have been hay and grain. Woodmorappe again goes through detailed calculations to conclude that 100,000 to 200,000 cubic feet was necessary to store "the 371-day supply of food for the 16,000 animals."

Woodmorappe's conclusions demand a few assumptions. But he is no more speculative than Robert Moore: "Noah needed large quantities of fresh, clean water, kept in troughs and inspected frequently. Where did this come from? How was it stored and distributed? Conditions being what they were, it must have splashed out of the troughs shortly after they were filled, mixed with food and waste to form a stinking, slippery swamp all over each deck, while the reserves were rapidly choked with algae to form an undrinkable swill."[37]

It would mean a lot of work for Noah and his family, but it would have been possible to fit sixteen thousand animals on the ark.

4. What did Noah feed the animals?

Hay, grains, meat, and a lot of we-don't-really-know-but-we-can-make-an-educated-guess.

The Bible says God told Noah to take food for his family and the animals. But it offers no details about what that food should be.

The most general answer about what Noah would feed the animals is plants—hay, grains, leaves. More animals are herbivores (plant eaters) and omnivores (eating both meat and plants) than are true carnivores (meat only eaters). Except for the polar bear, most bears, for instance, are omnivores. Cows, horses, rhinoceros, and elephants all eat grass and other plants.

Some say the problem comes with the huge amount of hay required for herbivores. Noah could have used a combination of grain, which is far less bulky, and hay, which could have been compressed before putting it on the ark. Fruits and vegetables could have been preserved for the voyage by drying, which would have also reduced their bulk, making them easier to store. Drying foods is not a modern technique. Claude Levi-Strauss, the father of modern anthropology, says the Aymara Indians of Bolivia were so skilled at dehydration of food that when the American army imitated their techniques, it "was able to reduce

71

the rations of powdered potatoes sufficient for a hundred meals to the volume of a shoe box."[38]

We don't really know how Noah fed the carnivores any more than we know how he fed the herbivores, but he could have done the same thing British whalers did in the eighteenth century. A whaling ship stopping at the Galapagos Islands—in the Pacific Ocean west of Ecuador—would take on between 500 and 600 giant tortoises, each one weighing as much as 660 pounds. "Whaling skippers were almost lyrical in their praise of tortoise meat, terming it far more delicious than chicken, pork or beef." These tortoises could hibernate in a ship without being fed or given water for a year or more.[39] As a good example of how an animal becomes endangered, so many tortoises were removed from the Galapagos Islands for food that giant tortoises almost became extinct by 1900. Noah could also have brought dried meat on board.

It's fascinating to discuss how Noah might have taken care of piscivores (animals that eat fish—for instance alligators and the bulldog bat), nectarivores (animals that eat the nectar of flowering plants—mostly insects and birds such as the hummingbird), frugivores (animals that primarily eat fruit—the orangutan's diet is usually 65 percent fruit), insectivores (animals that eat insects—for instance anteaters and frogs), live-food eaters such as snakes, and animals with specialized diets such as giant pandas, which eat bamboo, and koalas, which eat eucalyptus leaves. But nothing can be said with any certainty.

While speculating on how Noah might have fed the animals, it's fun to read a Jewish legend in which Shem, one of the sons of Noah, told Eliezar, the servant of Abraham, what it was like to feed the animals: "We had sore troubles in the ark. The day animals had to be fed by day, and the night animals by night. My father knew not what food to give to the little zikta. Once he cut a pomegranate in half, and a worm dropped out of the fruit, and was devoured by the zikta. Thenceforth, my father would knead bran, and let it stand until it bred worms, which were fed to the animal. The lion suffered with fever all the time, and therefore he did not annoy the others, because he did not relish dry food."[40]

Noah might have fed the animals primarily hay, grain, and both dried and fresh meat. Speculation about what he fed those animals with specialized diets gets into far more detail than we can talk about here and would not arrive at any conclusions anyway.

5. How did the animals breathe? Was there proper ventilation?
Since the Bible says apparently healthy animals left the ark after a year's stay, there must have been good ventilation.

The reason for asking this question is that the most traditional English Bible translation (the King James Version) says, "A window shalt thou make to the ark, and in a cubit shalt thou finish it above." This has been interpreted by some to mean that in a boat 450 feet long, 75 feet wide, and 45 feet tall, the only source of air and light was one tiny window 18 inches square. For instance, one blog quotes Ian Plimer, an Australian geologist and an outspoken critic of a global flood, as saying the ark had a "ventilation port of one cubit square so the atmosphere below decks was obviously indescribably fetid."[41]

But, Genesis 6:16 is the only place in the Old Testament where the Hebrew word translated "window" appears—so we don't really know what it means. And in Genesis 8:6 when Noah opened a "window," a different word is used, the standard Hebrew word for "window."

Another translation (the English Standard Version) translates Genesis 6:16, "make a roof for the ark, and finish it to a cubit above." It is more likely there was an opening—a series of windows—under the roof of the ark running along both sides.

Some writers have postulated the ark had flues—pipes that would be open to the air (with protection from rain) at the top of the ark and extend to the bottom of the interior. Cooler air from the outside would be drawn into the flues, warmed up by the animal heat inside the ark, and flow out the windows at the top of the ark. See, for instance, www.worldwideflood.com/ark/ventilation/ventilation.htm.

Others have speculated that the ark might have had one or more "moon pools" (See page 54) to aid the circulation of air as the water moved up and down.

Although the King James Version of the Bible talks about "a window" in the ark, there could have been many more openings that would have allowed adequate ventilation for animals and humans.

6. What did Noah do with all the waste generated by the animals?
We don't know.

John Woodmorappe estimates the animals on the ark would have produced twelve tons of waste a day. That's a lot of manure to dispose of! We don't know how Noah did it.

Genesis 8:1 says, "But God remembered Noah and all the beasts and all the livestock that were with him in the ark."

"Remember" here doesn't mean God did not forget Noah and the animals. It means God took care of them.

The same word *remembered* is used, for instance, in the story of Rachel later in Genesis. She had been married to Jacob for many years without children, which was a great stigma. But "then God remembered Rachel, and God listened to her and opened her womb. And she conceived and bore a son." God took care of Rachel.

As much as any of the questions about the animals—and about the ark itself—the question of waste management demonstrates that if you want to find an answer, it's possible to explain how Noah might have done it, even though a good answer takes a lot of ingenuity. But if you don't want find an answer, it's possible to point out the difficulties in a way that makes any solution sound impossible.

For instance, John Woodmorappe says,

> The key to keeping the enclosures clean was to avoid the need for Noah and his family to do the work.... One possibility would be to allow the waste to accumulate below the animals, much as we see in modern pet shops....
>
> Alternatively, sloped floors would have allowed the waste to flow into large central gutters. Noah's family could have then dumped this overboard without an excessive expenditure of manpower.
>
> The danger of toxic or explosive manure gases, such as methane, would be alleviated by the constant movement of the ark, which would have allowed manure gases to be constantly released. Secondly, methane, which is half the density of air, would quickly find its way out of a small opening such as a window....

75

While the voyage of the Ark may not have been comfortable or easy, it was certainly doable, even under such
unprecedented circumstances.[42]

On the other side, author Robert Moore, a proponent of the
impossibility of Noah's voyage, says,

> All authorities on animal care insist on the cleanliness of
> the stalls, urging the daily removal of waste and soiled
> bedding.... Creationists Balsiger and Sellier suggest that
> the bottom deck was used to store slurry, which accumu-
> lated to 800 tons during the voyage. However, a single
> adult elephant could produce 40 tons during this time,
> and there were many creatures even larger. Our average
> animal, the sheep, produces 0.34 tons per year; poultry,
> 0.047. Multiplying the number of vertebrates by 0.34,
> the seven pairs of birds by 0.047, yields 25,508 tons of
> waste—six times heavier than the ark itself! Of course,
> hibernation would greatly reduce this quantity, while the
> invertebrates and dinosaurs would add to it. Whatever the
> total, it would have been an awesome amount on the over-
> crowded boat, a breeder of infinite numbers of pathogens,
> and a source of noxious, choking fumes....
>
> Lamoureux's *Guide to Ship Sanitation* [says that] com-
> plex plumbing systems of pipes and pumps, air-gaps and
> back-flow valves, filters and chemical treatments are neces-
> sary.... Such technology was clearly beyond Noah's ability
> and the maintenance capabilities of his tiny crew; yet, if
> ever it was needed on a voyage, this was it.[43]

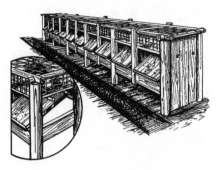

One way Noah might have simplified the disposal of waste from small animals would be with sloped floors under the cages that would empty into a manure gutter. This would be easier to clean than having to clean each cage. (courtesy of Answers in Genesis and used by permission)

Although the challenge of dealing with an estimated twelve tons of manure a day is one of the first questions people raise about Noah's voyage, the Bible offers no clues to how he did it. We don't know, although some have explained how it might be possible.

7. How did Noah and his family feed and water 16,000 animals?

We don't know, but some researchers say it's possible.

As we get into more details of the care of the animals, speculation and supposition abound. Those who believe Noah could not possibly care for the animals, point out its apparent impossibility. Those who believe it was possible, explain how Noah could have fed the animals.

Robert Moore says, "If each one received but one feeding during the voyage, and if all eight of the crew worked sixteen hours per day at the chore, each animal would wind up with just 44.3 seconds of attention during the entire year-long period! Some would have their meal on the first day, while others waited until they were nearly starved."[44]

However, John Woodmorappe says, "studies of non-mechanized animal care indicate that eight people could have fed and watered 16,000 creatures. The key is to avoid unnecessary walking around.... Don't work harder, work smarter."[45] He believes "many solutions to seemingly insurmountable problems are rather straightforward."

Noah could have used

- Gravity-fed automatic pet feeders, similar to those available at Petco, could hold enough food for a week.
- Water in the ark could be transported not with buckets but with pipes made of wood, bamboo, or other material.
- Hay, grain, and other foods were stored throughout the ark so they were near the animals, minimizing the amount of time necessary to feed animals or reload automatic feeders.

There's no question that feeding and caring for sixteen thousand animals for a year took most Noah's time and energy. We don't know how he and his family did it, but it might have been possible.

8. How did the animals get to the ark—especially from far away?
The animals came to Noah.

This answer begs the question, but it is what the Bible says.

God told Noah "to bring into the ark two of all living creatures, male and female, to keep them alive with you. Two of every kind of bird, of every kind of animal and of every kind of creature that moves along the ground will come to you to be kept alive,"[46] indicating the animals would come to Noah. Beyond that, everything is speculation.

People who don't think there were two (or seven or fourteen) of every kind of animal on the ark ask, not unreasonably,

- How could animals such as the Australian koala or the South American sloth get to the ark?
- How could Noah have figured out which animals were male and female?
- What happened to animals that cannot survive outside their environment, such as alligators, which live in wetlands?
- Did there need to be two of animals such as slugs and snails that do not have males and females?
- How did Noah accommodate animals that are used to living in extreme cold or in desert conditions?
- Wouldn't wild animals tend to panic when put in a closed space?

People who say bringing animals into the ark was possible postulate that before the Flood, there was one land mass, called Pangea, and all the continents were connected. They also point out that animals are able to sense danger and have been known to migrate to avoid it. One geologist claimed to have predicted the San Francisco earthquake of 1989 by studying lost pet ads, hypothesizing that the animals were fleeing the impending quake.[47]

Woodmorappe assumes Noah gathered animals into a menagerie in anticipation of the Flood and then God miraculously commandeered the animals, forcing them to leave their menagerie enclosures and go to the ark after Noah. God probably commandeered some wild animals as well.

Whether God brought the animals to Noah ahead of time or brought them to the ark just before the Flood, the Bible says God did it, although we don't know how.

9. How did the animals spread around the world after the Flood?

At great risk of sounding like a broken record…we cannot be sure how the animals got to remote parts of the earth.

God told Noah to "Go out of the boat with your wife, your sons, and their wives. Take all the birds and animals out with you, so that they may reproduce and spread over all the earth."[48]

That sounds pretty straightforward…until you start thinking about it. There is not much problem with birds because they can fly vast distances. But…

- How did the kangaroo and platypus get to Australia?
- How did the giant panda get to China?
- Why did the gila monster migrate to the southwestern U.S. instead of staying in a similar climate in the Middle East, near where the ark presumably landed?
- How did animals that live only in caves get to the caves from the ark?

There's no definite answer, of course. But suggestions are made such as

- migration
- land bridges
- log rafts
- lower ocean levels immediately after the Flood due to an assumed Ice Age
- people took some animals with them in their human migrations.

It is possible to explain the migration of animals throughout the world after the Flood, but the key, as explained by Paul Taylor, a British creationist, is you have to presuppose that the account in the Bible is true. "Opponents of biblical creation use similar models" and come to different conclusions, he says. "Animal migration around the world illustrates the goodness and graciousness of God." [49]

Mount Ararat, The Mountain of Pain (Wikipedia)

6.
ARARAT
THE MOUNTAIN OF PAIN

I t is awe-inspiring, treacherous, legendary, and one of the world's most famous mountains. Most mountains, even very tall ones, don't look quite so majestic because of other mountains around them. However, Mount Ararat—16,854 feet above sea level with Little Ararat next to it—rises nearly 12,000 feet above the semi-arid plains of eastern Turkey in one of the most politically sensitive places on earth. Ten miles to the east is the Iranian border; twenty miles to the north is Armenia (formerly part of the U.S.S.R.). The area has been inhabited by Armenians, Turks, and Kurds for thousands of years.

"In the seventh month, on the seventeenth day of the month, the ark came to rest on the mountains of Ararat." Is it possible the ark of Noah could still be there?

• • •

Throughout history, the mountains of Armenia have been identified as the resting place of Noah's ark. A first century BC Greek historian, Alexander Polyhistor, said the ark was "grounded in Armenia," where "some part still remains." Philostorgius, a fifth century church historian, said "Mount Ararat is…where, according to Scripture, the ark came to rest, and they say that considerable remnants of its wood and nails are still preserved there."[50] And in AD 610, Isidore of Seville, "the last scholar of the ancient world," said, "Ararat is a mountain in Armenia, where the historians testify that the ark came to rest after the Flood. So even to this day wood remains of it are to be seen there."

Armenia, one of the world's oldest civilizations, identified Ararat as the home of the gods, much as the Greeks revered Mount Olympus. According to Armenian tradition, angels protected the ark after the Flood, and pilgrims visited the ark to worship and remove small portions of wood as holy relics. Eventually, though, humankind became so wicked once more that God did not let even the righteous visit the ark, and it became buried in snow and ice. The secret location of the ark was passed down from Armenian father to Armenian son, along with a belief that near the end of the world the ark would be revealed as a reminder that people should turn from their wicked ways.

Ararat is such a treacherous mountain that its Turkish name, *Agri Dagh*, means "the Mountain of Pain." Blinding snowstorms, avalanches, deep crevasses, and volcanic scree make it a challenge to explore. Glaciers in places two hundred feet thick cover several square miles of the mountain. Poisonous snakes and scorpions add to the danger. And because Ararat sits by itself, it acts like a giant lightning rod. Bolts of lightning have immobilized

This engraving shows both Great Ararat with snow on the top and Little Ararat. (courtesy of www.noahsark.it and used by permission)

climbers and clouds are full of static electricity. John Morris, who explained in chapter 3 why he believes in a global flood, reported that when he climbed Ararat, "Our ice axes and crampons were singing, our hair was standing on end, even J.B.'s beard and my moustache were sticking straight out."[51]

A rock slide injured Apollo 15 astronaut Jim Irwin in 1982. Alone and with night approaching, he took refuge next to a huge boulder. Another rock slide then careened down Ararat and, according to his wife Mary, "enormous, jagged rocks whizzed by his head and sparks flew as rock slammed against rock sending hundreds of fragments ricocheting in all directions. Jim's rock held fast; he was safe for the night and slept."[52]

Dr. Almet Ali Arslan, who was born on the lower slopes of Mt. Ararat and has been climbing it since 1965, said, "Technically, the climb is not too difficult. But scientists have stated that there is active carbon dioxide on the upper slopes in addition to the normal lack of oxygen on extreme heights. This combination is very hard on climbers and causes illness and confusion.... Volcanic 'bombs,' rocks and solidified lava, roll down the mountain."[53] It's no wonder the Armenians say the top of the mountain is inaccessible. But throughout history people have tried to climb it.

The earliest story we have of a search for the ark occurred eighteen hundred years ago, first told by an Armenian historian[54] who lived about one hundred years after the event. Saint Jacob was appointed bishop of Medzpin in what is today southeastern Turkey. When he learned people in his area believed the ark had landed on Mount Judi, near where they lived, Jacob decided to provide evidence that it was elsewhere. Since Mount Masis, 200 miles north, was 2-1/2 times the height of Mount Judi, Mount Masis took on the name of Mount Ararat and became the focus of ark traditions.

Saint Jacob was a devout man who had the power to do miracles. As he started climbing Ararat, he prayed most fervently that God would allow him to see the ark. He became thirsty from fatigue, knelt to pray, and a spring of water appeared. Every day he would climb, fall asleep from exhaustion, and wake up the next morning at the bottom of the mountain where he had started. He repeated his efforts daily until finally an angel appeared to him and said because of his devout persistence, "The Lord gives ear to your prayer and grants what you desire." The angel gave him a piece of wood from the ark, which he carried down the mountain. "The inhabitants of the city came forth to meet him with boundless joy and happiness," said the historian, and eagerly accepted the gracious gift of the wood.

At the place where the angel gave him the wood, Jacob built a monastery, which stood for nearly fifteen hundred years until the early summer of 1840, when an earthquake and avalanche destroyed it. The wood the angel gave Jacob is still preserved in the Etchmiadzin Cathedral in Armenia, the oldest state-built church in the world.

One thousand years later, European travelers to Armenia told stories they heard from Armenian monks. Marco Polo, for instance, wrote, "In the central part of Armenia stands an exceedingly large and high mountain, upon which, it is said, the ark of Noah rested." A British scholar, John Kitto, visited Ararat in the 1830s and reported, "Many attempts were made in former times to attain the summit, access to which the native Armenians believe to be supernaturally forbidden; yet with strange incongruity, they sell to pilgrims relics from the wood of the ark, which is still believed to lie upon the summit."[55] Gradually, questionable Armenian stories morphed into undisputed fact.

One of the more interesting stories comes from Jan Janszoon Struys, a seventeenth century Dutch sailmaker and sailor who wrote a bestseller in 1676 with the not-so-snappy title of *The Voyages and Travels of John Struys through Italy, Greece, Muscovy, Tartary, Media, Persia, East-India, Japan, and other countries in Europe, Africa, and Asia*. Struys told of being forced to treat a hermit who was "sick with a rupture." For seven days Struys hiked up Ararat, each night staying in the hut of a different hermit. Each hermit provided a "man and donkey: the first as a guide and the other to carry our food and wood." Eventually

Struys arrived at a large room "hewn out of the rock" where the ailing hermit had lived for five years. Struys nursed the hermit back to health and, in appreciation, the hermit gave him "a cross which was made from the true wood of Noah's ark" and "a stone from the rock upon which the ark rests."

In 1829, a German scientist and mountaineer, Friedrich Parrot, was asked by Russian czar Nicholas I to explore Ararat, which he did with three Russian soldiers, four scientists, and a monk as an interpreter. It took three attempts, but the group became the first in modern times to reach the summit where, Parrot wrote, "no human being has ever been since the time of Noah." To memorialize the occasion they planted a cross they had carried with them. Armenian citizens did not believe Parrot and his companions could climb Ararat, which was forbidden by God, and so the climbers testified under oath that they had made it to the top.

A major earthquake on June 20, 1840, altered Mount Ararat and destroyed the monastery and chapel built by St. Jacob and the town of Akori. Sixty years later a British traveler and politician, H.B. Lynch, told of an eyewitness account of the earthquake: "He was thrown onto his knees by a sudden reeling of the ground.... Close by his side the earth cracked; a terrific rolling sound filled his ears." Four days later there was "a second and scarcely less momentous collapse. On this occasion a mass of mud and water burst from the chasm, as though some colossal dam had given way. Blocks of rock and huge pieces of ice were precipitated over the base, and the flood extended for a space of about thirteen miles.[56]

A Russian army officer who explored the area in the early 1900s lamented that the chapel built by St. Jacob had contained "many ancient relics of the epoch of Noah, many ancient manuscripts and books,"[57] but they were now buried.

The earthquake opened up the Ahora Gorge, which drops more than a mile, and after the earthquake more and more sightings of the ark have been claimed, many in or around the Ahora Gorge.

Once such story was told by Haji Yearam, who grew up at the foot of Ararat and heard shepherds and hunters occasionally tell of having seen one end of the ark. In 1856, when Haji was a teenager, three Englishmen who wanted to prove the legend of Noah's ark was a fraud hired his father as a guide, and Haji went with them. Because it was an unusually hot summer, when the party reached a little valley near the top, "they found the prow of a mighty ship protruding out of the ice. They went inside the ark and did considerable exploring. It was divided up into many floors and stages and compartments and had bars like animal cages of today. The whole structure was covered with a varnish or lacquer that was very thick and strong, both outside and inside the ship. The ship was built more like a great and mighty house on the hull of a ship, but without any windows. There was a great doorway of immense size, but the door was missing."[58]

The men went into a rage at finding what they hoped was nonexistent and told Haji and his father that if they breathed a word about the ark, the men would find them and torture and murder them. By the time he was 75, though, Haji was no longer worried about the Englishmen and wanted to clear his conscience by telling his story to someone.

Haji dictated his story in 1915 to Harold H. Williams, a Seventh-Day Adventist pastor in Oakland California, where they both lived. Harold moved to Massachusetts and in 1918 he saw a story in the local paper stating, "an elderly scientist on his death bed in London was afraid to die before making a terrible confession. It gave briefly the same date and facts that Haji Yearam had related in his story." Harold saved the newspaper clipping in the notebook in which he had written Haji's dictation, but in 1940, the notebook was destroyed in a fire, and in 1952 Harold reconstructed Haji's story as best he could remember it in a letter addressed, "To Whom It May Concern." It's an interesting story, but cannot be verified and depends on the accuracy of the memories of both Haji Yearam and Harold Williams.

In 1876, James Bryce, who would later become the British Ambassador to the United States, climbed Mount Ararat and told of his adventure in *Transcaucasia and Ararat*. Quoting an earlier traveler, he wrote, "the mountain is altogether uninhabited, and from the halfway to the top of all, perpetually covered with snow that never melts, so that all the seasons of the year it appears to be a prodigious heap of nothing."

At the 13,000-foot level, Bryce says he found a piece of hand-tooled wood about four feet long and five inches thick. The wood could have been part of the cross Friedrich Parrot had put on the top or part of a larger cross Russian Colonel J. Khodzko erected in 1850 when he spent five days on the summit. Or…some have said…it could be part of the ark itself. When Bryce's interpreter told the archimandrite of the monastery of Etchmiadzin that Bryce had been to the top of Ararat, "The venerable man smiled sweetly. 'No,' he replied, 'that cannot be. No one has ever been there. It is impossible.'"

90

Although Bryce believed the wood he had found was possibly part of the ark, he also pointed out, "Indeed, I have not found any author who says he has himself seen [the ark], though plenty who (like the retailers of ghost stories) mention other people who have."

That certainly seems to be the case in the twentieth and twenty-first centuries when Ararat has been searched by hundreds of "arkaeologists," all of whom believe the ark is there. But the critical evidence—a piece of wood, a photograph, a detailed report, an eyewitness—all seem to have been seen at one time, sometimes by many witnesses, but cannot now be found.

While most searchers for the ark explore Ararat, some believe the ark is elsewhere.

MOUNT JUDI

The story of Noah and the ark told in the Quran is similar to the story told in the Bible…with one notable exception.

The Bible says the ark came to rest "on the mountains of Ararat." According to this tradition, Noah and his family settled just east of Ararat in Nakhchivan (an area and a city in Azerbaijan you've probably never heard of). Nakhchivan is believed to mean "The place where Noah landed after the Flood." The tomb of Noah still stands there today.

The Quran—along with Jewish and Syriac traditions predating the Quran—says, however, the ark came to rest "on al-Judi,"

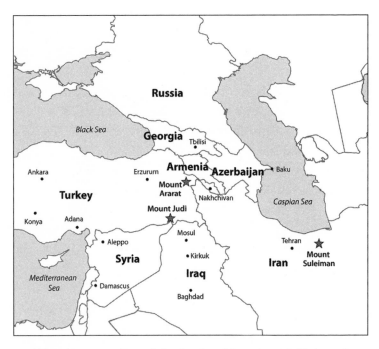

Although most people search for the ark on Mount Ararat in Turkey, others say the ark landed on Mount Judi in Turkey or on Mount Suleiman in Iran.

usually identified with Cudi Dagi, almost two hundred miles southwest of Ararat near the Turkish city of Cizre, which also has a tomb of Noah. The Mount Judi tradition seems most prevalent prior to AD 1300, at which time attention shifted to the larger Mt. Ararat. A monastery called the Cloister of the Ark built on Mount Judi's summit was destroyed by lightning in AD 766.

A thirteenth century geographer from Iran said wood from the ark was seen on Mount Judi as late as the eighth and ninth centuries, and that eventually most of it was taken off the mountain and used to build a monastery or mosque. However, Friedrich Bender, a German geologist searching for oil for a Turkish firm in the 1950s, claimed to have found wood on Mt. Judi in 1953 that was determined by radiocarbon dating to be about 6,500 years old.

Advocates of Mount Judi say "The mountains of Ararat" mentioned in Genesis refers to the entire mountainous region in Armenia between the Black and Caspian Seas, including Mount Judi.

IRAN

It was 1986 when Bob Cornuke first heard Ed Davis tell his remarkable story.

While stationed in Hamadan, in northern Iran, in 1943, U.S. army sergeant Ed Davis befriended an Iranian, who said his grandfather had visited the ark. A rock slide near his friend's village had diverted a stream and cut off the village's water supply.

Ed provided some dynamite to clear the rock slide, and in gratitude, Davis's friend's father offered to show him the ark.

In a shed by his house, the father showed Davis an old cage
door with bars made of woven branches, hand-carved latches,
ancient pottery, and more—all ark artifacts. After several days'
travel up a mountain in the unusually hot summer, they reached
a gorge. Looking over the edge, Cornuke reported that Davis
said he saw, "a huge, rectangular structure lying on its side, like
a battleship stuck on a sandbar. *Oh, my God!* thought Davis. *It's
enormous.*"59

Davis said he could see into the broken craft, its "intricate
interior design, comprising three distinct floors, stacked one on
top of another. Between floors lay a dense gridwork of frail-
looking partitions and narrow walkways."60

Although Cornuke later climbed Ararat several times, including once with astronaut Jim Irwin, he became convinced the ark
is not on Ararat for two reasons: (1) details given by Ed Davis do
not match Ararat and Davis said he didn't know what mountain
his friend's father had climbed. Hamadan is more than five hundred miles from Ararat. (2) The Bible indicates the descendants
of Noah traveled eastward to Shinar (Babylon). Ararat is north
of Babylon.

So Cornuke began searching in northern Iran. Twice he
climbed Mount Sabalan, the second highest mountain in Iran
and near the eastern side of the Caspian Sea. He found nothing.

In 2005, Cornuke and two others climbed the 15,300-foot
Takht-i-Soleiman ("The Throne of Solomon"), a mountain on
the southern rim of the Caspian Sea. Here he found features
matching the description given by Ed Davis. At 12,500 feet, they
found a "massive formation." Parts of it "looked like the petrified

remains of an old Spanish galleon. The dark rocks had a burnished look with what appeared like bark and other wood-like characteristics."[61]

"I'm not about to make a dogmatic pronouncement about what we found on Mount Suleiman," Cornuke said. "But I can say that I have a high level of confidence that it was the same thing that Ed Davis saw.... I don't intend to try to convince anyone of anything. I'm happy to share what I've found and let other people draw their own conclusions."[62]

If Bob Cornuke is right, Noah's ark is not on Mount Ararat in Turkey, but on Mount Suleiman in northern Iran.

7.
ARKAEOLOGISTS
SEARCHING FOR THE ARK

When an earthquake buried several villages on the slopes of Mount Ararat in 1883, the Turkish government sent an expedition to investigate. According to one report, the Turkish scientists and soldiers and a British diplomat "came upon a gigantic structure of very dark wood, embedded at the foot of one of the glaciers, with one end protruding.... Effecting an entrance through one of the broken corners, the explorers found it filled for the greater part with ice, the interior partitioned off into compartments."

No news release or report from Turkey of this expedition has ever been found. The quote above is from a British magazine, *Prophetic Messenger*. However, the discovery was reported—with some scorn—in the *New York Herald*, the *Chicago Tribune*, the *New York World*, and other papers. Just as modern urban legends make the rounds, the source for the American papers' stories was probably *Prophetic Messenger*, retold without verification. The

Count Kalnoky's presence. The Emperor William confered the Order of the Black Eagle upon him, the highest Prussian decoration.

NOAH'S ARK
DISCOVERED ON MOUNT ARARAT.

LONDON, Aug. 9.— [Special Cable.]—A paper at Constantinople announces the discovery of Noah's ark. It appears that some Turkish Commissioners appointed to investigate the question of avalanches on Mount Ararat suddenly came upon a gigantic structure of very dark wood protruding from a glacier. They made inquiries of the inhabitants. These had seen it for six years, but had been afraid to approach it because a spirit of fierce aspect had been seen looking out of the upper window. The Turkish Commissioners, however, are bold men, not deterred by such trifles, and they determined to reach it. Situated as it was among the fastnesses of one of the glens of Mount Ararat, it was a work of enormous difficulty, and it was only after incredible hardships that they succeeded. The ark, one will be glad to hear, was in a good state of preservation, although the angles—observe, not the bow or stern—had been a good deal broken in its descent. They recognized it at once. There was an Englishman among them who had presumably read his Bible, and he saw it was made of the ancient gopher wood of Scripture, which, as every one knows, grows only on the plains of the Euphrates. Effecting an entrance into the structure, which was painted brown, they found that the admiralty requirements for the conveyance of horses had been carried out, and the interior was divided into partitions fifteen feet high. Into three of these only could they get, the others being full of ice, and how far the ark extended into the glacier they could not tell. If, however, on being uncovered it turns out to be 300 cubits long it will go hard with disbelievers in the Book of Genesis. Needless to say, an American was soon on the spot, and negotiations have been entered into with the local Pasha for its speedy transfer to the United States.

to is expected at Cape Haytian. A great battle was fought before Jeremie, in which the Government troops were completely defeated. Seven of their Generals were taken and executed. The revolutionists are marching on Leogane. The Government is therefore raising the siege of Miragoane and covering Port-au-Prince, establishing its headquarters at Leogane.

THE FRENCH.
IN TONQUIN.

LONDON, Aug. 9.—The Times correspondent at Hong Kong says he has been informed there are no Chinese troops either in Tonquin or on the frontier, but that the garrisons in the provinces of Yun Nan and Kwang Si have been secretly increased. Much grain and rice is being stored at Canton. The impression prevails that China is playing a waiting game, which is costing the French much and the Chinese little.

IN MADAGASCAR.

PARIS, Aug. 9.—Admiral Pierre, whose conduct at Tamatave towards the British Consul and others caused much feeling in England, asks to be replaced forthwith, owing to the poor condition of his health.

Letters from Madagascar say Shaw, the British missionary, was arrested for concealing two Hova spies.

LONDON, Aug. 9.—The Government deem the latest dispatches from Madagascar so satisfactory that they will no longer hold the transports Himalaya and Orontes in readiness for immediate service.

PARIS, Aug. 9.—It is reported that 3,000 French reinforcements will be sent to Madagascar and 600 to Reunion.

M'DERMOTT.
WHAT IS KNOWN OF THE MAN IN NEW YORK.

NEW YORK, Aug. 8.—[Special.]—There is no doubt that the man McDermott who was arrested in Liverpool is James McDermott, of Brooklyn, who has always been noted as a good deal of a blatherskite. In connection with the news of his arrest Mr. Paul Murphy, of No. 165 East Thirty-fifth street, and who is a worker in the Irish cause, related the following story today of a plot concocted by Mc-

The article on "Noah's Ark discovered on Mount Ararat" in the August 10, 1883 edition of *The Chicago Tribune* was only one article in several papers to report this news received by "Special Cable" from London.

Chicago Tribune article concluded, "Needless to say, an American was soon on the spot, and negotiations have been entered into with the local Pasha for the speedy transfer [of the remains of the ark] to the United States."

The twentieth century saw an explosion of expeditions searching for Noah's ark. Travel had become easier and interest in the ark had become more intense. The biggest obstacles to exploration were political and physical. The government of Turkey was reluctant to hand out too many permits to climb Ararat and the physical challenges of the climb could not be overcome, even with modern equipment.

An inspiration for many modern arkaeologists was a realtor in New Mexico, Eryl Cummings, who, in 1945, read a magazine article about the discovery of Noah's ark. Over the next forty-four years Eryl himself climbed Ararat sixteen times and encouraged dozens of ark searchers. "There have been thirty-seven expeditions since 1961," he said in 1976, "and I'm familiar with practically all the expeditioners. I don't know any one of them who has been successful."[63] John Morris and John Warwick Montgomery both credit Eryl Cummings and his wife Violet as being an encouragement to them. It was Eryl Cummings who heard the story of Haji Yearam (told in chapter 6) in 1952, made it known to ark searchers, and then spent years following leads to confirm the details. In 1973, Violet, herself an accomplished researcher, wrote a popular book, *Noah's Ark: Fable or Fact?* Most of the following stories have been researched by or have a connection with Eryl and Violet Cummings.

During World War II, the U.S. military made hundreds of flights from Tunisia in North Africa, directly over Mt. Ararat, supplying provisions to troops at the Russian air base in Yerevan, Armenia—at the time part of the Soviet Union. In 1943, two American pilots saw what they thought looked like a huge ship and later took an Air Force photographer on a supply run. His pictures and an accompanying story were said to have been published in the Mediterranean edition of *Stars and Stripes,* one of the dozens of editions of the U.S. Armed Forces newspaper.

Many veterans remember seeing the article, but it has never been found. One said the *Stars and Stripes* article caused such a sensation on his base that the French chaplain preached a sermon about Noah.

"As an Air Force G.I., I had been astounded by the story printed in *Stars and Stripes* about the 8th Air Force crewmen flying out of Tunisia who had looked out of their B-17 to see the ark nestled among the crags and glaciers of Ararat," said Tim LaHaye, co-author of *The Ark on Ararat.*

Violet Cummings told of a visit by Homer Wyman who remembered the picture and article and had saved it. Then, "he explained how only a couple of weeks before, his wife had transferred all his wartime mementos from the worn old scrapbook into a brand-new album for a homecoming surprise.... But, like all the other tattered, yellowed old clippings, it did not take kindly to a transplant, and not realizing the value of the article on the ark, she had thrown it away."[64]

There have been stories of other pictures of the ark, but strangely, none survive.

George Greene, an oil and pipeline engineer working in Turkey, took pictures in 1953 of what he claimed to be the ark. He showed his portfolio of clear eight-by-ten-inch black-and-white photos to dozens of people in an effort to form an expedition to explore the mountain. George's pictures showed the prow of a boat protruding from a morass of brush, mud, stone, and large chunks of ice. The joints and horizontal planks were clearly visible on one side. George Greene never got back to Turkey, and in 1962, he either accidentally fell to his death or was murdered in British Guiana.

In trying to find George's photos and maps, Eryl Cummings and others interviewed thirty people who confirmed they had seen the pictures. One even drew a crude representation of what the ark and the area around it looked like in the photos. Another of George Greene's friends thought he might have the photos in a manila envelope in his garage with Greene's other effects. But the garage was vandalized only ten days before Eryl's visit and the photos have never been found.

A pilot who flew a 1974 secret U.S. Air Force mission to photograph what might be Soviet-made defense installations said, "I can tell you what I saw with my own eyes. It was a dark, black foreign object about two-thirds of the way up the mountain near a gorge. It was oblong and partially buried in ice, overhanging a cliff. To me, it certainly looked like a boatlike object." The film containing the pictures the pilot took was kept by the Air Force and classified Top Secret.[65]

• • •

Between 1952 and 1955 a French industrialist, Fernand Navarra, made three climbs up Mount Ararat.

One evening before their first climb, Navarra and his four companions were approached at a café in Igdir, a town on the northwest side of the mountain, by an elderly man who had heard of their search and told them, "The ark is still there! This I was told by the greybeards, and they were told it equally by those who were old during their youth. And all of us here believe it. All the people of Igdir, Bayazid, or Yerevan, to the last shepherd on the twin mountains, all believe it. And we shall hand that belief to our children, with the bounden duty of passing it on to their descendants.... To reach it [the ark] one must be as pure as a newborn child...."[66]

On the first climb, Navarra and his team found buried under some ice a dark form, "unmistakenly the shape of the ship's hull," according to *The Forbidden Mountain*, which he wrote about his experiences. Navarra's second climb, made alone in the summer of 1953, was unsuccessful due to harsh weather.

On the third climb in 1955, "a warm year," Navarra and his eleven-year-old son found, forty feet under the Parrot Glacier, a five-foot hand-hewn wooden beam he claimed to be from the ark. It was heavy and they had to cut it and were able to bring only a portion down the mountain. The portion was certified to be about five thousand years old by the Forestry Institute of Research and Experiments of the Ministry of Agriculture in Spain, although others have dated Navarra's wood as being much younger. The head of UCLA's isotope laboratory said radiocarbon tests indicated that the wood was only about 1,230 years old, and the National Physical Laboratory of Teddington, England dated it at about 1,190 years old.[67] Navarra received quite a bit of publicity and wrote a second book, *Noah's Ark: I Touched It*.

Fernand Navarra holds a piece of wood he and his son found on Ararat in 1955 at the 13,500-foot level that he says is a piece of the ark. You can watch him make his discovery on youtube. (courtesy of www.noahsark.it and used by permission)

Videos of Navarra and his son on the mountain discovering the ark can be seen at www.youtube.com/watch?v=EMV6MmcgMjw, a five-minute segment from the 1993 film, *The Incredible Discovery of Noah's Ark.*

Navarra climbed Mt. Ararat twice more in 1968 and 1969 under the auspices of The Search Foundation. The explorers returned from their expeditions with several small pieces of wood similar to the wood Navarra found in 1955. The Foundation said it made no claim "as to the identity of the artifact," but they hoped further exploration would identify the wood as part of Noah's ark. Navarra's guide later accused him of buying the wood in a nearby village and carrying it up the mountain, although the guide's claim cannot be verified.

Former astronaut James Irwin led two expeditions to Ararat in the 1980s. He was kidnapped once, and was not able to find any tangible evidence of the ark. "I have done all I possibly can," he said, "but the ark continues to elude us."

The search continues. Donna D'Errico, former *Playboy* playmate and *Baywatch* star, nearly fell to her death in 2012 climbing Ararat. "I'm going back," she said. Bruce Feiler, author of *Walking the Bible*, took a film crew to Ararat and interviewed a man who claimed he had fallen into a hole on top of a glacier and had found a piece of the ark. Joanna Lumley, a British actress and star of *Absolutely Fabulous*, searched Ararat in 2012 because, "It's something that's fascinated me all my life."

The last one hundred years have been filled with almost-but-not-quite stories—accounts of people who explored Ararat but didn't find anything; of people who took pictures of the ark, but the pictures are lost; of government reports that are buried—intentionally or accidentally—in Russian, American, or Turkish files. With such interest in the ark, there is a temptation to create hoaxes, and a few of those exist as well.

In the end, for those who believe the ark still exists, there are enough stories, drawings, and even pieces of wood to justify their belief. Eryl Cummings found encouragement in the stories he investigated: "The stories have come at different times, from people of different walks of life, from different countries; yet the stories pretty well coordinate when describing the positioning and condition of the ship."[68]

But for those who don't believe the ark still exists or ever existed, there are enough questions in each report to justify their skepticism.

APPARENT HOAXES

Opportunity for fame and fortune creates opportunity for scams, frauds, and self-deception. The search for the ark is no exception. The stakes are high. "The discovery of Noah's ark would be the greatest archaeological find in human history," Melville Bell Grosvenor, National Geographic Society president, is reported to have said. Here are four of the better-known fake ark sightings.

VLADIMIR ROSKOVITSKY

In 1916, Vladimir Roskovitsky of the Russian Air Force saw the ark while flying over Ararat. When he reported his sighting, the Tsar ordered two engineering companies to Ararat. They found the ark, took measurements, drew up plans of it, took photographs, and sent their report to Tsar Nicholas II. Nicholas abdicated the next spring, the courier who delivered the report was executed, and the report itself has never been found. Possibly it was destroyed.

It's a great story. But it's 95 percent fiction written by an "off-center man" with an "exaggerated imagination." In the 1930s a retired lawyer named Benjamin F. Allen had heard "vague reports" by two Russian soldiers who had participated in the exploration of Ararat and the alleged discovery of Noah's ark. He mentioned this information to his neighbor, Floyd Gurley, who wrote the story and published it in *New Eden Magazine* in Los Angeles. Vladimir Roskovitsky is the creation of Gurley's imagination. The story may have a kernel of truth in it, but it's mostly fiction.

GEORGE JAMMAL

After seeing *In Search of Noah's Ark* by Sun International, actor George Jammal, as a joke, wrote Dr. Duane Gish of the Institute for Creation Research about his own efforts to find Noah's ark with his associates, "Mr. Asholian" and his son-in-law "Alis Buls Hitian." Although the names are clear giveaways to the joke, no one got it, and when Sun International wanted to do an expanded version of its highest-grossing film for broadcast on CBS, it contacted George. He played along.

He found a piece of wood by a railroad track in Long Beach, California, boiled it with ketchup, teriyaki sauce, perfume, and then baked it in an oven. Holding this "piece of Noah's ark," George Jammal told forty million viewers on prime-time television he and his companion, "Vladimir Sobitchsky," had crawled through a hole in the ice on Mt. Ararat, and found the ark. Unfortunately Vladimir backed up to take a photograph, fell, and died in an avalanche.

When he heard CBS was planning two more programs with Sun International, George Jammal revealed his hoax.

THE DURUPINAR SITE

The most widely read article about the discovery of Noah's ark appeared in *Life* magazine, September 5, 1960.

Heavy rains and three earthquakes in 1948 exposed a formation that looked remarkably like a boat at the "Durupinar site," eighteen miles south of Ararat's summit. The uniqueness of the formation was discovered by Turkish army captain Ilhan Durupinar when he studied photos taken for NATO in 1959. The next year an expedition conducted by the Archeological Research Foundation (ARF) visited the site. After much digging inside the boat-shaped formation, the group concluded, according to their press release, "there were no visible archaeological remains" and this formation "was a freak of nature and not man-made." In spite of ARF's conclusion, *Life* published pictures from the expedition with the headline, "Noah's Ark? Boatlike form is seen near Ararat." So far, there was nothing fraudulent or dishonest about the publication of Durupinar pictures—just a little misleading.

The Durupinar site was largely ignored until 1977, when Ron Wyatt, a former nurse anesthetist, adventurer, and self-taught archaeologist from Madison, Tennessee, began promoting it as the site of Noah's ark. In spite of his efforts to convince others including James Irwin and John Morris that Noah's ark was at the Durupinar site, he found few to agree with him.

Was Wyatt merely overenthusiastic or a fraud? Probably the latter. He made extravagant claims such as saying the Durupinar site contained "trainloads" of gopherwood. In addition to the ark, he claimed to have found the location of Sodom and Gomorrah, the site of the Tower of Babel, and the place where the Israelites crossed the Red Sea. He even claimed to know where the ark of

FROM THE AIR the ship-shaped outline lies in the center of a landslide on the slope of a mountain that is only 25 miles from the Russian border. The landslides are of recent origin, may have packed thick mud and stones around the strange form. The photo was shot by a Turkish aerial survey plane from 10,000 feet.

NOAH'S ARK?

Boatlike form is seen near Ararat

While routinely examining aerial photos of his country, a Turkish army captain suddenly gaped at the picture shown above. There, on a mountain 20 miles south of Mt. Ararat, the biblical landfall of Noah's Ark, was a boat-shaped form about 500 feet long. The captain passed on the word. Soon an expedition including American scientists set out for the site.

At 7,000 feet, in the midst of crevasses and landslide debris, the explorers found a clear, grassy area shaped like a ship and rimmed with steep, packed-earth sides. Its dimensions are close to those given in Genesis: "The length of the ark shall be 300 cubits, the breadth of it 50 cubits, and the height of it 30 cubits," that is, 450x75x45 feet. A quick two-day survey revealed no sign that the object was man made. Yet a scientist in the group says nothing in nature could create such a symmetrical shape. A thorough excavation may be made another year to solve the mystery.

FROM THE GROUND, at the "stern," the 160-foot-wide object is seen to have grass-covered mound in center. The 20-foot-high ties dwarfs expedition's horses.

112

CONTINUED

In 1960, *Life Magazine* showed pictures of a "boat-shaped form" the size of the biblical ark on Mount Ararat with the tantalizing headline, "Noah's Ark?" "A quick two-day survey revealed no sign that the object was man made," the article said. "Yet a scientist in the group says nothing in nature could create such a symmetrical shape."

the covenant was (the one Indiana Jones searched for). And yet, scientists, historians, and biblical scholars dismiss his claims. The Garden Tomb Association (Wyatt claims the ark of the covenant is in a chamber on the grounds of the Garden Tomb in Jerusalem.) says it "totally refutes the claim of Mr. Wyatt."

NOAH'S ARK MINISTRIES

In 2010, Noah's Ark Ministries International (NAMI), based in Hong Kong, announced at two press conferences it had found the ark on Mount Ararat, put pictures of the find on Youtube— proclaiming, "The Discovery of the Ark: Actual stills and footage" —and reported that carbon dating suggested wood samples taken from the ark were about forty-eight hundred years old.

However, NAMI admitted that no one with the organization "had ever seen a 'large wooden structure,'" and the photos it was showing had been given to it by Parasut, a Kurdish guide "we trust." When Carl Wieland of Creation Ministries International in Australia reported this, he said that he "is distressed that once more, it seems the Christian world is being 'set up' by another heavily hyped, but phony archaeological claim."[69]

Randall Price, who was part of NAMI in 2008, said that in 2008 and 2009 wood from "an old structure in the Black Sea area" was planted at the site on Ararat by "ten Kurdish workers hired by Parasut." Price said he thinks the structure is a hoax perpetrated by the Kurdish guide and his partners to extort money from the Chinese evangelical Christians, although he stressed this is only his opinion.

"To make a long story short, this is all...a fake,"[70] Price said.

That woodpecker has to go. (courtesy of Ramon Teja and used by permission)

8.
NOAH GOES TO HOLLYWOOD

The old adage that says the book is usually better than the movie is frequently true. The director may have a different take on the story (Stephen King didn't like Stanley Kubrick's screen adaptation of his book *The Shining*). A book lets readers picture the characters and setting with their own imagination; movies have to make everything too specific. (*The DaVinci Code* describes its main character, Robert Landon, as looking like Harrison Ford; in the movie Landon is played by Tom Hanks.) Movies are not able to tell the whole story because they don't have time.

The old adage may have been true of *The Shining, The DaVinci Code*, and *Harry Potter* books. It's certainly true of the story of Noah and the ark. The story in the Bible is one of God's grieving because of humankind's sinfulness, of His decision to destroy the world because of man's wickedness, of Noah's faith in God, and of God's providing a way for humans and animals to "Prosper! Reproduce! Fill the earth!"[71]

The story of Noah and the ark has been filmed many times for theater and television and usually the biblical story is a framework on which the writer and director hang their own story with their own viewpoint.

NOAH'S ARK (1928)
Written by Darryl F. Zanuck; Directed by Michael Curtiz

Thomas Edison invented both the phonograph and the motion picture camera in the 1800s, but it wasn't until the 1920s that sound and sight were combined into talking pictures. There was no shortage of silent feature films about biblical subjects. *The Ten Commandments* (1923) and *Ben-Hur* (1925) were among the ten top grossing silent films in the U.S. In 1926, Warner Brothers introduced "Vitaphone," a system combining sound and images, and the next year released the first commercially successful sound film, *The Jazz Singer*. It was the dawn of the talkie, but first there were part-talkies in which some scenes were silent, while others had sound.

The year following *The Jazz Singer*, Warner Brothers released a part-talkie that was the most expensive film in its history to that time: *Noah's Ark,* starring Dolores Costello and George O'Brien. It was truly a major motion picture, and eventually made back twice its more than $1 million cost. "Three years in the making…a cast of ten thousand…the most overpowering scenes ever filmed."

The primitive special effects were marvelous. Huge curtains of water splashed down on hundreds of "pagans" fleeing the Flood.

Mighty structures crumbled as "the spectacle of the ages unfolds as a tidal wave of power."

In reality, the climactic flood scene was a dangerous shoot. Cameraman Hal Mohr thought it would put untrained extras in jeopardy and quit over it. And he was right. The amount of water was so overwhelming that three extras drowned, one had to have his leg amputated, and a dozen suffered broken bones and serious injuries. Two of the extras in that flood scene later became stars: John Wayne and Andy Devine.

Although the promotion focused on the biblical Flood, the movie told two stories, a favorite approach of film epics of the 1920s. The modern story was typically inspirational and moralistic; the ancient story was from the decadent past.

After an amazingly moralistic opening that drew a parallel between the greed of those who worshipped the golden calf and the modern stock market—interestingly, the movie opened one year before the market's 1929 crash—*Noah's Ark* tells a love story set in World War I. Our hero, Travis, a young American playboy living in France, falls in love with a German girl, Marie. They marry, and he rescues her from a firing squad when she is accused of being a German spy. They are then trapped in a building that is hit by artillery. A minister compares the blood of modern war to the world before the time of the Great Flood.

The film then flashes back to the time of Noah with the main characters of the World War I love story playing characters in the Noah story. An evil officer in the Russian Secret Service becomes King Nephilim, who orders the sacrifice of a beautiful virgin (Marie). She is rescued by Japheth (Travis), Noah's son, and they are on the ark as all around them people are drowning, including King Nephilim.

Noah's Ark is epic and dramatic. But don't look to it for biblical accuracy. The story of the golden calf in the Bible had nothing to do with Noah. It appears as if Darryl Zanuck, who wrote the story, relied more on Cecil B. DeMille's *Ten Commandments* (the 1923 version) than on Scripture! Somehow elements of the story of Samson and the story of the Israelites in Egypt make their way into Zanuck's flood story. When Noah hears from God, he walks up a mountain, encounters a burning bush, and God zaps two giant tablets in the side of a mountain with words. The tablets turn like the pages of a book. Then Noah responds to God's instructions on how to build an ark with words from the Lord's prayer in the New Testament: "Thy will be done, on earth as it is in heaven." One blogger describes all this as "endearingly goofy."[72]

FATHER NOAH'S ARK (1933)
Walt Disney Productions; Directed by Wilfred Jackson

From 1929 to 1939 Walt Disney Productions created seventy-five animated shorts called Silly Symphonies. They are wonderfully creative because Disney used them to train young animators and test new styles, effects, and technologies. Donald Duck got his start in a Silly Symphony.

This eight-minute film, "Presented by Mickey Mouse" according to the title frame, uses the story of Noah to focus on the animals and lots of sight gags. The animals help Noah build the ark—monkeys chop down trees and a rhino cuts them into planks while a woodpecker pounds wooden nails. The elephant

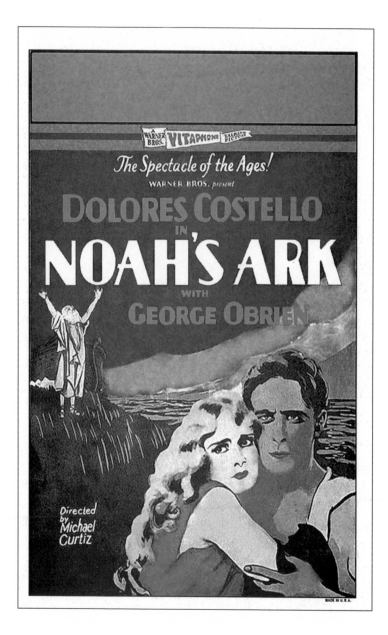

cannot fit through the ark's door until a lightning bolt strikes a stubborn donkey, who leaps on the ark, hits the elephant, pushes him through the opening, and the door is shut.

As you might expect, the film has a bouncy, fun feel, completely oblivious to the destruction of all living things caused by the Flood.

CAPTAIN NOAH AND HIS MAGICAL ARK (1967-1994)
WPVI-TV, Philadelphia

For more than twenty-five years W. Carter Merbreier, an ordained Lutheran minister, and Patricia, his wife, starred as Captain and Mrs. Noah in a Philadelphia children's show, *Captain Noah and His Magical Ark*. At its height, the daily program was syndicated to twenty-two markets across the U.S. and in the 1970s it was watched by more children in Philadelphia than *Sesame Street* and *Captain Kangaroo* combined.

The show's standard fare was a lot of cartoons and interaction with puppets such as Wally the Walrus and Maurice the Mouse. There were guests, too, such as Elvis Presley, Charles Barkley, Jon Stewart, and Martina Navratilova. Jim Henson came on *Captain Noah and His Magical Ark* to introduce Kermit the Frog to Wally and Maurice. Frank Perdue, president and promoter of one of the largest chicken farms in the U.S., demonstrated the miracle of baby chicks hatching.

Captain Noah and His Magical Ark ran from 1967 to 1994, when the Merbreiers decided to retire. They were both inducted into the Philadelphia Broadcast Pioneers Hall of Fame in 2001.

EVAN ALMIGHTY (2007)
Screenplay written by Steve Oedekerk; Directed by
Tom Shadyac

Biblical epics are usually expensive, especially when animals and floods are involved. *Evan Almighty* is not a biblical epic, but at a cost of $175 million, it is the most expensive comedy film ever made. Starring Steve Carell as Evan Baxter and Morgan Freeman as God, it was developed as a sequel to *Bruce Almighty*, a successful 2003 release starring Jim Carrey as Bruce Nolan.

In a funny sense, the story line of *Evan Almighty* follows the biblical story of Noah more closely than either Michael Curtiz's *Noah's Ark* or Darren Aronofsky's *Noah*.

Evan Baxter, a successful news anchor in Buffalo, New York (In *Bruce Almighty*, Evan had beat out Bruce Nolan for the Buffalo job.), wins one of New York's congressional seats by promising he will change the world and moves to northern Virginia. When he prays that he might actually change the world, animals start following him around two by two, he grows a beard that reappears whenever he tries to shave it, and ancient tools are delivered to his house.

Then God appears to Evan and tells him to build an ark, reminding him he wanted to change the world and this would let him at least save his town, if not the world. At first, Evan's wife supports the idea, and their three sons help Evan build the ark. (The ark built for the movie was the actual size given in the Bible—450 feet long, 80 feet wide, and 51 feet high.) When she thinks Evan is beginning to go insane, it takes a conversation in a diner with God himself to get her to again help Evan prepare for a flood.

(Courtesy of Universal Studios Licensing LLC)

On the appointed day, the animals enter the ark, the rains begin, a shoddily built dam above Prestige Crest, the town where Evan lives, bursts, and the ark floats through the flooded streets of Washington, D.C., coming to rest in front of the Capitol (Capitol Hill isn't as impressive as Mt. Ararat, but it's not bad), where Congressman Evan Baxter is able to turn the tide on a Public Land Act, proposed by the same crooked congressman who built the defective dam.

God appears again to Evan and tells him the real way to change the world is to do one Act of Random Kindness (A.R.K.) at a time. Everyone except the crooked congressman lives happily ever after.

NOAH (2014)
Written by Darren Aronofsky, Ari Handel, and John Logan;
Directed by Darren Aronofsky

Darryl Zanuck told the story of Noah and the Flood as a flashback in a love story that showed the blood and violence of World War I. Steve Oedekerk set the story of Noah in modern suburban Washington, D.C. Darren Aronofsky makes a very different adaptation. He said his story is "about environmental apocalypse. Noah was the first environmentalist."

Noah stars Russell Crowe as Noah, Jennifer Connelly as his wife, Anthony Hopkins as Methuselah—Noah's cave-dwelling grandfather—and Emma Watson as Noah's adopted daughter. "Rediscover the epic story of one man and the most remarkable event in our history," a trailer said.

Aronofsky's interest in Noah goes back to when he was thirteen and won a United Nations competition for his poem about the end of the world as seen through Noah's eyes. "That story has interested me ever since." With collaborator Ari Handel, Aronofsky published in 2011 a French-language graphic novel that told their story of God's choice of Noah to save the planet. He then used the graphic novel to help sell the film to Paramount. The French publisher described the story this way…

His name is Noah…. He looks like a Mad Max out of the depths of time. In the world of Noah, pity has no place. He lives with his wife and three children in a land barren and hostile, in the grip of severe drought. A world marked by violence and barbarism….

But Noah is like no other. This is a fighter and also a healer. He is subject to visions which announce the imminent end of the earth, swallowed by the waves of an endless deluge…. If man is to survive, he must end the suffering inflicted on the planet and "treat the world with mercy." However, no one is listening.

The tyrant Akkad, who Noah went to visit in the city of Bal-llim, chased him and sentenced him to flee. After consulting with his grandfather Methuselah, Noah decided to rally to his cause the terrible Giants and accomplish the task entrusted to him by the Creator.

The world of Aronofsky's Noah is a bleak one—the earth is scorched, devastated by man's disrespect for the environment. Unlike others, Noah and his family live off the land and "heal it as best we can." His animal hospital cares for wounded animals and those who survive evil poachers. The trees, the animals, the environment—"All God created is dying." Noah has recurring dreams of a flood and seeks advice from his grandfather, Methuselah. To get to his cave, Noah has to go through the land of the Watchers, fallen angels who are eleven feet tall with six arms—and appear on the cover of the graphic novel.

Methuselah tells Noah that God has chosen him for a reason and that he should respond with obedience and courage. He gives Noah a magic seed that grows into a forest, which Noah cuts down to build the ark, having enlisted the help of the Watchers. The animals come to the ark two by two, and the rains start.

Noah decides the only reason God preserved him and his family is to make sure the animals on the ark return to the earth safely. If mankind disappeared, "it would be a better world." His family should have no more births so that humans will eventually die out and then "the creatures of the earth, the world itself, shall be safe." But one of his daughters-in-law is pregnant. If it is a boy, Noah will let it live; but if it is a girl, it will be killed. The woman gives birth to twin girls and Noah sets out to kill them both while the animals on the ark help pin down his family. But he is too weak to carry out his task. "I can't do it," he says to himself and to God. "I am sorry."

The movie concludes with his daughter-in-law asking Noah to teach his grandchildren "about the world around them and how to live in it…. Maybe if you give them your wisdom, they will do better with their world than we did with ours."

This description is adapted from a summary by movie critic and screenwriter Brian Godawa, one of the few outsiders to read the script by the fall of 2013.[73] Godawa points out that "in the script, what God cares about is the environment, not so much man. As Noah reveals, 'The world squirms beneath our foot, a poisoned husk. The Creator sees this, He mourns it, and will tolerate it no longer. He would (rather) annihilate all in an instant than watch this creeping rot…. We must treat the world with mercy so that the Creator will show us mercy.'"

Filming began in the fall of 2012, first in New York, where two massive arks were built—one in a Brooklyn soundstage and one in Oyster Bay. Oyster Bay, however, was right in the path of superstorm Sandy, which hit hard on October 29, 2012. Since the 450-foot long ark was not designed to be seaworthy, production had to be halted. Emma Watson tweeted, "I take it that the irony of a massive storm holding up the production of *Noah* is not lost." The ark inside Brooklyn's New York Armory was not damaged.

Why was *Noah's* budget $150 million? For one thing, all the animals are digital creations. "We had to create an entire animal kingdom," said Aronofsky. "All the animals in the movie are slightly tweaked; I didn't want the clichéd polar bear, elephant, and lion walking onto the ark; I didn't want the shot of a giraffe's head looking over the rail…. We basically went through the animal kingdom and pinpointed the body types we wanted: some pachyderms, some rodents, reptiles, and the bird kingdom. We chose the species and they were brought to life with different furs and colors. We didn't want anything fully recognizable but not completely absurd either."

The result includes the most complex scene ever created by the amazing artists at Industrial Light & Magic.

"I don't care how many Bible stories or translations you've read," said film critic and screenwriter Drew McWeeny, "and I don't care how many films based on those stories you've seen. You have never seen anything like what Darren Aronofsky has planned for *Noah*."

Noah's Ark Park and Resort, next to the magnificent Tsing
Ma Bridge, Hong Kong (HK Arun, Wikipedia)

9.
WHERE CAN YOU SEE THE ARK?

There is nowhere in the United States where you can see a life-sized replica of the ark. You have to go to the Netherlands, Hong Kong, or Canada. But a spectacular ark is coming to Kentucky!

JOHAN'S ARK IN DORDRECHT, HOLLAND

Johan Huibers was a carpenter and a successful contractor in northern Holland who became a Christian when he was twenty-four years old. He wholeheartedly embraced his new faith and served others by building wells in Ethiopia and doing relief work in Albania and Bosnia. He wanted to do more, but he wasn't sure how.

One night, after watching a terrible North Sea storm hammer the dikes near his house, he had a dream—it must have

A 450-foot long replica of the ark opened for visitors in July, 2012, in Dordrect, Holland. The huge boat is seaworthy and has a restaurant, a movie theater, an ampitheater, and meeting rooms. It was built by Johan Huibers, a Dutch contractor who believes, "If you have faith, anything is possible"—even a life-sized fully operational ark.

been a nightmare—of a fierce storm causing the ocean to wash over Holland. When he saw a book on Noah's ark the next week, he realized he could share his faith by building a replica of the ark. At first his wife, Bianca, thought he should stick to building wells in Ethiopia. But Johan did not give up his dream.

"In the past most people went to church and heard the Word on Sundays," Johan said. "Now they don't go to church any more, so to reach them, God uses other means."

In 2005, he began to build a half-size (220 feet long) ark. He worked on his own for a year and then got help from his son and volunteers—not unlike the original Noah. He even sawed his own planks from 1,200 trees.

Johan's half-sized ark opened to the public in 2007 with a coffee shop, play area, and exhibition room. There was a place where children could build a miniature town and then watch as it was destroyed in a flood. For more than three years, the half-sized ark traveled the canals of Netherlands, carrying horses, lambs, chickens, rabbits, and other animals, and stopping at twenty-one mooring places to "give children something tangible to see that Noah's ark really existed," and "to tell them there is a God who loves us." But Johan Huibers had bigger dreams!

After selling his half-sized ark, Huibers built a full-sized one, 450 feet long. Made of Swedish pine reinforced with steel, it weighs three thousand tons and opened to the public in July, 2012. It has a restaurant, a movie theater, an ampitheater, and meeting rooms—and one hundred thousand visitors the first year, which was enough to let Huibers break even financially.

Looking "across the ark's main hold, a huge space of stalls supported by a forest of pine trees, visitors gaze upon an array of stuffed and plastic animals, such as buffalo, zebra, gorillas, lions, tigers, bears, you name it. Elsewhere on the ark is a petting zoo with actual live animals that are less dangerous or easier to care for—such as ponies, dogs, sheep, and rabbits—and an impressive aviary of exotic birds."[74]

The full-sized ark now towers above the flat Dutch landscape in Dordrecht, just south of Rotterdam, welcoming visitors and hosting conventions. Johan wanted to sail it to the London Olympics in 2012, but could not get all the safety code clearances in time. He would like to take it to Rio de Janeiro for the 2016 Olympics.

Johan Huibers is working on a new dream, one even bigger than his first: he wants to get Israelis and Arabs to cooperate to build a water pipeline from the Mediterranean Sea to the Dead Sea.

"If you have faith," he says, "anything is possible."

NOAH'S ARK PARK AND RESORT, HONG KONG

Thomas Kwok, joint chairman and managing director of Sun Hung Kai Properties, a real estate development firm in Hong Kong, is, with his two brothers, the third richest person in Hong Kong and, according to Forbes, the twenty-sixth richest in the world. His company built the 118-story International Commerce Center, the tallest building in Hong Kong.

Thomas became a Christian when he went through an eleven-week Alpha Course, a program that seeks to introduce people to the basic tenants of the Christian faith. "My wife and I were so touched…we decided to be baptized the following Christmas," he said.[75]

In the early 2000s, Sun Hung Kai began to develop Ma Wan, a 240-acre island in the Hong Kong harbor, by building a five-thousand-unit apartment building and a family-oriented amusement park with rides. Because of Thomas's Christian faith, he convinced his brothers to build a life-sized replica of Noah's ark as part of the Ma Wan Park to "promote education and interest as well as love and harmony." And the biblical account of creation.

Unlike Johan's ark in Holland, which is seaworthy, the ark in Hong Kong was never intended to float. It's a stationary building billed as "the world's first full-scale ark replica" and sits under the busy and magnificent Tsing Ma Bridge, which connects Hong Kong with the city's airport.

The five-story life-sized ark with a fine dining restaurant and banquet hall on the ground floor is the centerpiece of Noah's Ark Park and Resort. The bottom floors of the building also contain an "Ark Expo"—displays, dioramas, a children's creation museum—while the top floor contains a forty-three-room hotel. The plan was to install a rainbow using light refraction, but the technology to pull it off was too difficult. Then the park manager realized the water jets used to spray hanging plants in the park created a mist that refracted light at certain hours of the day, creating rainbows. Real ones.

It took one hundred builders nearly three years to construct the ark. The surround-sound theater brings the opening scenes of the Flood to life with a vibrating floor and sprays of water. An Ark Garden includes sixty-seven pair of fiberglass animals. "There are few family recreational options in Hong Kong," said a park representative. "This presents family-friendly values, including teaching about earth's functioning, and to love the environment."

"When you go to Disneyland, there's really no message there," said one visitor. "But at Noah's ark, there is such a strong message that life goes on."

"The attraction has made a big splash amongst Hong Kong's youngsters," said one reviewer, "while also coming in for criticism for its hidden creationist message…. Whether you believe in creationism or not, the grand size of the Noah's ark exhibition is undeniably impressive, especially set, as it is, underneath the equally impressive Tsing Ma Bridge."[76]

THE SCHOOL OF THE SPIRIT, FLORENCEVILLE, NEW BRUNSWICK, CANADA

Paul Smith's father started a church in New Brunswick in 1945, and since 1979, father and son have been working together. They have pastored the Burnham Road Cathedral, started a Bible school, supported missionaries…and built an ark two-thirds the size of Noah's. The Canadian ark is 300 feet long, 36 feet wide, two stories high, and sits on top of a small hill just outside Florenceville. It makes no pretense at being seaworthy.

The ark contains dormitory rooms for students in the Bible school, administrative offices, and healing rooms where people in need of healing can "stay in one of the rooms and be immersed in God's presence…by listening to soft music and reading of Scriptures," according to the church's website. It's also used as a retreat center.

Although a life-sized replica of the ark has not been built in the United States, several have been started.

FROSTBURG, MARYLAND

For nearly forty years a life-sized replica of the ark has been under construction in Frostburg, a town in the mountainous western part of Maryland. Richard Greene, pastor of a non-denominational church, said that in 1974 God told him in repeated dreams to build an ark on a hillside next to Interstate 68. Groundbreaking was in September 1974 and steel beams for the first phase were installed twenty-five years later. The church—now named God's Ark of Safety Ministry—is raising money to finish the first phase, and the pastor has been around the world to raise money for the project. "As God provides, we will build."

When completed, the building will be a church and conference center. The purpose is to be a "sign that Jesus is coming soon." Richard says he has not lost confidence, even though the ark is still a skeleton of concrete and steel. Referring to other replicas of the ark, he added, "If I got jealous of what other people are doing, this whole thing would have sunk years ago. You just keep on keeping on…. But if God doesn't move a lot quicker, I won't be around to see the completion of this ark."

WILLIAMSTOWN, KENTUCKY

Ken Ham believes God created the world in six literal days. Questioning this belief, he says, is "an erosive legacy" that has "filtered down from Christian seminaries and colleges to pastors—and finally to parents and their children," resulting "in a generation of young people leaving the church."

Born in Australia, where he founded the Creation Science Foundation, Ken moved to the United States and, with two friends, founded what is today called Answers in Genesis. The mission of Answers in Genesis is to "support the church" and "bring reformation by reclaiming the foundations of our faith"—including the belief in a six-day creation.

In Australia Ken had a dream to build a creation museum, a dream that came true in May, 2007, when Answers in Genesis opened a seventy-thousand-foot state-of-the-art museum in Petersburg, Kentucky (just west of the Cincinnati airport). It includes animatronic dinosaurs, a live petting zoo, a Stargazers Planitarium and Johnsonian Observatory, the largest zip line in the Midwest, and an insectorium that "rivals the quality of the Smithsonian's display."

It also contains displays about Noah's ark. A full-scale cross-section of the ark demonstrates details of how Noah might have built it. An animatronic Noah answers pre-programmed questions ("Why did I build the ark? Well, I built the ark because, simply put, God told me to!"). A Flood Geology Room contains videos, dioramas, and exhibits to explain a global flood. Other exhibits show how Noah and his family might have cared for the animals and lived on the ark.

Nearly two million visitors have gone through the Creation Museum since it opened in 2007. When a consulting firm estimated 1.6 million people would visit a replica of the ark the first year and when 43 percent of people responding to a 2009 survey by *60 Minutes* and *Vanity Fair* said they would like to see the ark, Answers in Genesis began work on Ark Encounter.

Set on eight hundred acres about forty-five minutes from the Creation Museum, Ark Encounter will be a theme park with a life-sized ark, which is expected to be the largest timber-frame structure in America, as its centerpiece. Eventually the park will also contain a Walled City, the Tower of Babel, a first-century Middle Eastern village, a boat ride down the Nile, an aviary, a petting zoo, and more.

When visitors board the ark they can see a blacksmith making metal fittings, a sawmill cutting timbers, a pitch pot, and a rope-making machine.

The basic planning is completed, and the design team, headed by Patrick Marsh (See interview starting on age 56), is working on the details. The construction contract with an Indiana firm has been signed, and $24.5 million funding is being raised. In December, 2012, *The Atlantic* reported more than $8 million had

Ark Encounter, an 800-acre theme park to be built just south of the Cincinnati airport in Williamstown, Kentucky, will feature a life-sized ark built by Amish craftsmen. Future attractions will include a Walled City, the Tower of Babel, a first-century Middle Eastern village, and a walk-through aviary. Ark Encounter is being built by Answers in Genesis, which also built the Creation Museum about 45 minutes northwest of Ark Encounter.

been raised. One year later, the figure was almost $15 million.

"When I asked Michael Zovath (head of Ark Encounter) whether his project was really achievable," said the *Atlantic* writer, "—whether he could safely and efficiently fabricate a multimillion-dollar tourist attraction to God's specifications, using only wooden pegs, planks, beams, and whatever else might have been available to Noah—he didn't hesitate. 'It's certainly possible,' he said. 'It was done a few thousand years ago.'"

None of the following ark-related experiences are where you can see an ark, but you might find them interesting.

SIGHT AND SOUND

"A visit to Sight & Sound Theatres is truly a unique experience. Story, song and spectacular staging bring the Bible to life. With professional actors, trained animals, special effects, and memorable music, Sight & Sound shows inspire more than 800,000 guests every year."

If you think that description sounds like an advertisement, you're right. It's from the official Lancaster County, Pennsylvania website. But it's an accurate description of a two-thousand-seat theater in Ronks, Pennsylvania. Since 2008, Sight & Sound has also operated in a similar venue in Branson, Missouri.

For nearly forty years, Sight & Sound has staged such productions as *The Splendor of Easter, Joys of Christmas, Daniel and the Lions' Den, In the Beginning, Joseph*…and *Noah—the Musical.* The Noah stage show ran in 1995-6, from 1998 to 2001, in 2004, and most recently from March to November, 2013. A return engagement has not yet been scheduled.

"The show is fantastic," said one visitor. "I still can't get over how so many of the animals came on stage—unaided—and knew right where to go!"

NOAH'S ARK WATER PARK

You can find Congo Bongo, Black Thunder, Point of No Return, and Quadzilla waterslides, and the Big Kahuna wave pool at Noah's Ark Water Park in Wisconsin Dells. But no ark. The gift shop built to look sort of like an ark was destroyed by an electrical fire in 2012.

Noah's Ark Water Park, with fifty-one water slides, claims to be the largest water park in the United Sates. It has nothing to do with Noah or the ark except the name.

BUY YOUR OWN ARK

Be the first kid on your block to own your very own ark…a model ark, of course. Dens Model Ships in central Pennsylvania has a number of model arks available. One is nearly five feet long and comes with thirty-two pairs of animals; there are several dioramas; a "construction model" shows how the ark was built. For more details see:

www.scalednoahsarkmodels2buy.redtienda.net.

10.
NOAH'S SECRET FOR
SURVIVING THE END OF THE WORLD

We don't have to worry about the world's being wiped away by another flood. "Never again will everything living be destroyed by floodwaters," God told Noah. "No, never again will a flood destroy the earth."[77] Noah's earth-destroying Flood was the first and the last.

But a flood is not the only way the world could end. Some potential global disasters lurking in the future are a nuclear holocaust, either created on purpose or by accident; an agricultural crisis caused by an exploding population leading to massive starvation; effects of global warming such as rising sea levels and an increase in the frequency and severity of extreme weather such as hurricanes and typhoons.

Stephen Petranek, editor-in-large of the Weider History Group, explained at a TED Conference, "Ten Ways the World Could End." Four of his more fascinating are...

1. **The earth is hit by an asteroid.** In 1908, a two-hundred-foot piece of a comet exploded over Siberia and flattened forests for a hundred miles. It had the effect of one thousand Hiroshima bombs. In 1989 a large asteroid passed directly through Earth's orbit, missing us by six hours. "This is not a question of if, but of when, and how big."

2. **The earth meets a rogue black hole.** There are about ten million dead stars in the Milky Way, and each of these stars is a black hole that gobbles up everything around it, including light. If the earth were to get within one billion miles of a black hole, its orbit around the sun would become elliptical, which means for three months our surface temperatures would go up to 150 to 180 degrees and for three months they would go to 50 degrees below zero. "That won't work too well."

3. **A new global epidemic decimates our population.** Germ mutations are not unusual, but if one mutates so that it is resistant to antibiotics, it could sweep through nations with devastating effect. It's happened before. In 1918, a flu epidemic in the United States killed twenty million people—one in five in the country. The bubonic plague killed 30 percent of the population of Europe in the fourteenth century.

4. **Reversal of the earth's magnetic field.** Believe it or not, this happens every few hundred thousand years and we're overdue. When a reversal occurs, the earth loses its magnetic field for about one hundred years. The magnetic

138

field protects the earth from cosmic rays and particles streaming at us from the sun. "Basically, we would fry," Petranek said.

The Bible also seems to predict a violent destruction of the earth sometime in the future, but describes it in more poetic terms. The visions and imagery in the Book of Revelation are difficult to understand in their details, but dramatic and encouraging in the big picture. Towards the end of the book, seven angels pour out the wrath of God on the earth. And some of these predictions sound similar to those of Stephen Petranek.

- "Loathsome, stinking sores erupted."
- "The sea coagulated into blood, and everything in it died."
- "Rivers and springs...turned to blood."
- "Fire blazed from the sun and scorched men and women."
- "Mad with pain, men and women bit and chewed their tongues."
- "The great Euphrates River...dried up to nothing.... The kings of the whole world" prepared for war.
- "Lightning flashes and shouts, crashes and a colossal earthquake. Every island fled and not a mountain was to be found. Hailstones weighing a ton plummeted, crushing and smashing men and women as they cursed God for the hail."[78]

When Noah was warned of disaster, God told him how to survive the Great Flood. What can we do now to survive the end of the world? How can we take action to save people, save plants, and save animals?

139

SAVING PEOPLE

The *Daily Mail* reported in 2006 that theoretical physicist and cosmologist Stephen Hawking said, "The long-term survival of the human race is at risk as long as it is confined to a single planet. Sooner or later, disasters such as an asteroid collision or nuclear war could wipe us all out. But once we spread out into space and establish independent colonies, our future should be safe…. My next goal is to go into space. Maybe Richard Branson will help me."

The first step to space colonization—a modern day equivalent of the ark—is relatively cheap and available space travel. The Russian space program put the first human into space and the American space program put the first human on the moon. But these programs were neither cheap nor available, and Russian and American governments have lost their passion for space travel.

Private enterprise has picked up the slack. "In the history of mankind, 531 people have visited space so far," said George Whitesides, CEO of Richard Branson's Virgin Galactic. "We will fly [more people than that] in our first year of operation." He anticipates flying tens of thousands of flights in less than a decade. We will "fundamentally recast human beings' relationship with the space frontier."[79] Civilian space travel is here now.

Virgin Galactic will be able to take Stephen Hawking into space, but not all the way to Mars. Yet. Virgin Galactic is offering two-hour suborbital space flights for $200,000 each, which is cheap compared with the twenty to thirty-five million dollars a handful of people have already paid for up to two weeks on the International Space Station. The Virgin Galactic flights will launch from Spaceport America, which opened in 2011 in the New Mexican desert near the White Sands Missile Range. Spaceport America, the first of at least ten spaceports under construction around the world, is "designed to unlock the potential for space for everyone," its website says—at least everyone with an extra $200,000 lying around. Virgin's inaugural flight will be broadcast live on NBC when Richard Branson and his two adult children take its first commercial flight into space sometime in 2014.

Virgin Galactic is not the only company launching commercial space flights. Space Adventures arranges for tourists to go to the International Space Station. SpaceX, started by PayPal co-founder Elon Musk, has carried cargo to the International Space Station and hopes to start passenger trips in 2015. Blue Origin, the company of Amazon's Jeff Bezos, has completed a launchpad-escape test, but has not revealed its plans for passenger flights. Budget Suites of America owner, Robert Bigelow, plans to build his own space stations.

Apollo 14 astronaut Edgar Mitchell explains, "Space exploration must be undertaken not only out of simple human curiosity but also to further the survival of the species…. Many of our magnificent technologies, through design, ignorance, or misuse, are capable of destroying life as well as enhancing it. Space exploration alone holds the promise of eventual escape from a dying planet, provided we wisely manage our resources in the meantime and actually survive that long."[80]

We can take steps now to prepare for space colonization so that people can survive the end of the world.

SAVING PLANTS

The summer sun never sets in northern Norway, "The Land of the Midnight Sun." Three hundred miles *north* of Norway's mainland, nearly half way to the North Pole, is one of the most remote places on earth—Spitsbergen, an island the size of Ireland. Twenty-five hundred people live in Spitsbergen—as do 2,500 polar bears.

Four hundred feet inside a sandstone mountain on Spitsbergen is something that sounds as if it is out of a James Bond movie. The Svalbard Global Seed Vault has dual blastproof doors with motion sensors, two airlocks, and walls of steel-reinforced concrete three feet thick.

Food varieties are becoming extinct all over the world explains Charles Siebert, writing in the *National Geographic*. "In the United States an estimated 90 percent of our historic fruit and vegetable varieties have vanished. Of the seven thousand apple varieties grown in the 1800s, fewer than a hundred remain. In the Philippines thousands of varieties of rice once thrived; now only up to a hundred are grown there. In China 90 percent of the wheat varieties cultivated just a century ago have disappeared."[81]

Instead of growing thousands of locally adapted varieties of food, we have become increasingly dependent on a handful of varieties that offer increased yields—the miracle of the "Green Revolution," which has saved a billion people from starvation in the last fifty years. But if disease or climate change eradicates the few varieties on which we have come to depend, we will need to call back those varieties we've stopped using.

That's where 1,400 seed banks across the world come in. If disaster or disease threatens a plant, the plant can be started again from the seed bank.

Sometimes, however, local banks are not secure. After the U.S. invaded Iraq, for instance, looters destroyed a seed bank containing ancient varieties of wheat, lentils, and chickpeas. The Svalbard Global Seed Vault opened in 2008 to serve as a backup in the event of a local problem or a large regional or global crisis.

Nicknamed the Doomsday Seed Vault, it acts like a safe deposit box in which Norway owns the vault, but each local seed bank that sends samples to Spitsbergen owns the contents of its box. It has received nearly 800,000 unique seed samples out of almost two million different seeds in seed banks around the world. It contains thirty-two varieties of potatoes from Ireland, mold-resistant beans from Colombia, and nearly every kind of soybean developed in the U.S. in the last century.

It is the "Noah's ark of seeds," says conservationist Cary Fowler, former executive director of the Global Crop Diversity Trust, which operates the Svalbard Global Seed Vault. The Trust has launched a ten-year program of searching worldwide for those seeds not yet deposited in Spitsbergen. "This is an insurance policy we know we need."[82]

"Without seed we would be empty-handed and without the ability to produce food," adds Norwegian Minister of Agriculture and Food, Trygve Slagsvold Vedum. "The seeds frozen in the mountains of Svalbard may help to adapt our crops to changing climatic conditions and be an important key to global food security,"[83]

We can take steps now by saving samples of every known seed so that plants can survive the end of the world.

SAVING ANIMALS

We don't need an asteroid or rogue black hole to eradicate animals on the earth. We're doing it very nicely ourselves.

> In January 2012, a hundred raiders on horseback charged out of Chad into Cameroon's Bouba Ndjidah National Park, slaughtering hundreds of elephants.... Elephant poaching levels are currently at their worst in a decade.... From the air the scattered bodies present a senseless crime scene—you can see which animals fled, which mothers tried to protect their young, how one terrified herd of fifty went down together.[84]

From an estimated 27 million African elephants two hundred years ago, there are today fewer than half a million. And in 2012, a cover of *National Geographic* proclaimed that 25,000 were killed last year for their ivory.

LionAid estimates that fifteen thousand wild lions remain in Africa, compared with two hundred thousand thirty years ago.

Several species (but thankfully not all) of bumblebees in the United States have declined "substantially" over the last twenty to thirty years according to a survey, with one kind of bumblebee plummeting 96 percent.

Orangutans are at the "brink of extinction," according to the *National Guardian*, as the result of hunting and deforestation. In Borneo, there are an estimated 54,000 orangutans, half as many as twenty-five years ago. In Sumatra there are only seven thousand orangutans left.[85]

Three kinds of rhinoceroses (two-horned, black, and Javan), two kinds of whales (blue and sperm), and the Asian elephant are all among the top one hundred globally endangered animals.

What causes an animal to become extinct or endangered? Destruction of their environment, pollution, pesticides, disease, introduction of predatory animals, and hunting are all factors.

We can take steps now so that animals can survive until the end of the world, steps such as…

- Protect wildlife habitats. Deforestation, farming, and development all threaten particular animal species. Deforestation, for instance, is what is killing orangutans on Borneo.
- Reduce the threat of invasive species. Asian carp, a fast-growing, aggressive fish introduced to fish ponds in the southern U.S. in the 1970s, escaped when the Mississippi River flooded, and are making their way to the Great Lakes, where they would push native fish out of their habitats.
- Minimize the use of pesticides and herbicides.

In 2012, Rodolfo Almira, Reniel Aguila, Manuel Guerra, and Osmar Oliva from Hialeah, Florida, became concerned about the environment and the needs of animals, and wanted to create a safe environment where unwanted animals could find care, where injured animals could be nurtured back to health, and where people could adopt animals as pets. Taking their cue from the Bible, they joined forces to build "the Hidden Ark"—a five-hundred-foot-long replica of Noah's ark, with a veterinary clinic, stables, garden, petting zoo, and coffee shop.

"We're using Noah's ark to make a statement about helping animals and conserving our planet," said Carolina Peralta. "God teaches us to protect the animals."

It took the four friends only six months to build the first of three decks. Then county officials notified them they did not have the necessary permits and zoning approval (something the original Noah never worried about) and would have to tear down what they had built. The partially finished ark was removed in June, 2013, but their dreams got bigger—one hundred times bigger than their plans for the original five-acre site.

The four are now planning a five-hundred-acre park that will include modern rides, Babylonian gardens, a water park, and, of course, a replica of Noah's ark. You cannot have a Noah's Ark Amusement Park without it.

SAVING YOURSELF

Futurists and scientists encourage us to prepare for the end of the world by taking steps now to save people, save plants, and save animals. The Bible also encourages us to prepare now for "the end of the age"—and the story of Noah and the ark is involved. We should listen carefully to what the rocks say about the past—they don't lie—and we should listen carefully to what the Bible says about the future—it doesn't lie.

Jesus made the connection between Noah and the end of the age and He told His followers how to prepare for it.

When His disciples pointed out the magnificent Temple in Jerusalem, Jesus said, "You see all these, do you not? Truly, I say to you, there will not be left here one stone upon another that will not be thrown down." The Temple Jesus and His disciples were talking about was a huge structure built by Herod the

Great, who wanted his memory to live forever in the buildings he erected. The Temple was his masterpiece. Jesus said it would be torn down.

Herod's Temple was destroyed a few years later in AD 70 during the siege of Jerusalem by the Roman army led by Titus, who later became emperor.

After predicting the Temple's destruction, Jesus told His disciples that He would return to earth "on the clouds of heaven with power and great glory" at "the end of the age." Jesus, who calls Himself "the Son of Man," drew a parallel between the "days of Noah" and "the end of the age," making the point that no one will know when He will come back to earth:

> No one knows, however, when that day and hour will come.... The coming of the Son of Man will be like what happened in the time of Noah. In the days before the flood people ate and drank, men and women married, up to the very day Noah went into the boat; yet they did not realize what was happening until the flood came and swept them all away. That is how it will be when the Son of Man comes.... Watch out, then, because you do not know what day your Lord will come.... You also must always be ready, because the Son of Man will come at an hour when you are not expecting him.[86]

Noah spent sixty to eighty years building the ark, all the time urging people to change their violent, immoral, corrupt, and lawless ways because God was going to send destruction. No one believed him. They went on doing what they always did—eating, drinking, marrying, and carrying on with life, oblivious to the coming Flood. It will be like that, Jesus said, just before "the coming of the Son of Man."

After watching Noah for so many years without anything happening, the people grew tired of listening to his warnings and ignored him. "He's a guy who falls deeply into an obsession, and presses on long after it's become clear to everyone around him that the sane thing to do would be to quit,"[87] wrote Angie Han for Slashfilm, reflecting—probably without knowing it—what the people before the Flood thought about Noah.

The Apostle Peter also mentioned the Flood in a letter he wrote when he explained what it will be like just before the future coming of Jesus:

> You need to know that in the last days, mockers are going to have a heyday…. "So what's happened to the promise of his Coming? Our ancestors are dead and buried, and everything's going on just as it has from the first day of creation. Nothing's changed."
>
> They conveniently forget that long ago all the galaxies and this very planet were brought into existence out of watery chaos by God's word. Then God's word brought the chaos back in a flood that destroyed the world. The current galaxies and earth are fuel for the final fire. God is poised, ready to speak his word again, ready to give the signal for the judgment and destruction of the desecrating skeptics.[88]

It's not a pretty picture, but neither was Noah's Flood, as Darren Aronofsky's film shows.

Noah's secret on how to survive the end of the world is to watch, be ready, and choose now which side you are on...who you will believe and serve. Popular author C.S. Lewis explains,

Christians think [Jesus] is going to land in force; we do not know when. But we can guess why He is delaying. He wants to give us the chance of joining His side freely. I do not suppose you and I would have thought much of a Frenchman who waited till the Allies were marching into Germany and then announced he was on [the Allies'] side. God will invade.... When that happens, it is the end of the world. When the author walks on to the stage the play is over. God is going to invade, all right, but...this time it will be God without disguise; something so overwhelming that it will strike either irresistible love or irresistible horror into every creature. It will be too late then to choose your side.... It will be the time when we discover which side we really have chosen, whether we realized it before or not. Now, today, this moment, is our chance to choose the right side. God is holding back to give us that chance. It will not last forever. We must take it or leave it.[89]

As Joshua, a leader of the Israelites, said, "Choose this day whom you will serve." Be ready for the end of the age.

"Yes indeed! I am coming soon!" said Jesus at the very end of the Bible.

"So be it. Come, Lord Jesus! May the grace of the Lord Jesus be with everyone."[90]

NOTES

INTRODUCTION

1. David R. Montgomery, *The Rocks Don't Lie* (New York: W.W. Norton & Company, 2012), 9, 77.

2. Thomas H. Huxley, *Science and Christian Tradition* (London: Macmillan, 1893), quoted in David R. Montgomery, *The Rocks Don't Lie*, 177.

3. Henry M. Morris and John C. Whitcomb, Jr., *The Genesis Flood* (Philadelphia: The Presbyterian and Reformed Publishing Company, 1961), 117.

4. Bernard Ramm, *The Christian View of Science and Scripture* (Grand Rapids: Wm. B. Eerdmans Publishing Co., 1954), back cover.

5. Morris and Whitcomb, *The Genesis Flood*, 118.

6. www.answersingenesis.org/articles/nab3/flood-global-or-local

7. Robert A. Moore, "The Impossible Voyage of Noah's Ark," *Creation/Evolution Journal*, Vol. 4, Issue 11, Winter, 1983, 1.

8. "About This Issue," *Creation/Evolution Journal*, Vol. 4, Issue 11, Winter, 1983.

9. NOAH FOUND GRACE IN THE EYES OF THE LORD, Words and Music by Robert Schmertz, TRO-© Copyright 1951 (Renewed) Ludlow Music, Inc., New York, NY. International Copyright Secured. Made in U.S.A. All Rights Reserved Including Public Performance for Profit. Used by Permission.

1.

NOAH AND HIS FLOATING ZOO

10. Genesis 6:5, The Message.
11. Although the term "Watchers" in the Book of Enoch refers only to fallen angels, Daniel 4 refers three times to "a watcher, a holy one"— in verses 13, 17, and 23. Jude 6 seems to refer to the story in the Book of Enoch and the fate of the angels who "left their proper dwelling."
12. Enoch 106:18.
13. Quran 7:59.
14. Genesis 7: 11-12, The Message.
15. Genesis 7: 21-23, The Message.
16. Genesis 9:11, The Message.
17. Genesis 8:22, The Message.
18. Genesis 9:6-7, The Message.
19. Genesis 9:19, NKJV.
20. Sermon delivered at Dexter Avenue Baptist Church, Montgomery, Alabama, on November 4, 1956.
21. Hebrews 11:7, GNT.

2.

FLOOD STORIES AROUND THE WORLD

22. Irving Finkel, department head at British Museum, on *Noah's Ark: The Real Story,* a 2003 BBC video.
23. Shatapatha Brahmana
24. www.icr.org/articles/view/570/270

3.
WATER, WATER EVERYWHERE

25. William Ryan and Walter Pitman, *Noah's Flood: The New Scientific Discoveries about the Event that Changed History* (New York: Simon and Schuster, 1999), 15-17.
26. David R. Montgomery, *The Rocks Don't Lie*, 11.
27. John. D. Morris, *The Global Flood* (Dallas: Institute for Creation Research), 2012.
28. David R. Montgomery, *The Rocks Don't Lie*, 201, 203.

4.
HOW BIG WAS THE ARK?

29. *Noah's Ark: The Real Story*, BBC, 2003.
30. http://en.wikipedia.org/wiki/Chinese_treasure_ship

5.
THE ANIMALS WENT IN TWO BY TWO

31. Art Linkletter, *Kids Say the Darndest Things* (New York: Pocket Books, 1959), 78.
32. Genesis 7:2-3, NKJV.
33. Gen. 8:19, 17 NIV.
34. A website that claims to refute "pseudoscience," the "anti-science"

movement," and "crank ideas," and, according to the *Los Angeles Times*, "by their own admission engage in acts of cyber-vandalism."

35. http://creation.com/how-did-all-the-animals-fit-on-noahs-ark#endRef7

36. http://theconversation.com/we-have-species-thanks-to-noahs-ark-19542

37. Robert A. Moore, "The Impossible Voyage of Noah's Ark," 29.

38. *The Savage Mind*, Claude Levi-Strauss (London: Weidenfeld and Nicolson, 1966) 43.

39. "Floreana History—Pre 1900's," http://divingthegalapagos.com/the-galapagos-islands/floreana-history-pre-1900s, posted July 28, 2009.

40. Louis Ginzberg, "Noah and the Flood in Jewish Legend" in Alan Dundes, ed., *The Flood Myth* (Berkeley: University of California Press, 1988), 331.

41. www.jmm.org.au/articles/13377.htm

42. John Woodmorappe, "Caring for the Animals on the Ark" in *A Pocket Guide to Noah's Ark* (Petersburg, Kentucky: Answers in Genesis), 56-57.

43. Robert A. Moore, "The Impossible Voyage of Noah's Ark," 29.

44. Robert A. Moore, "The Impossible Voyage of Noah's Ark," 27.

45. John Woodmorappe, "Caring for the Animals on the Ark," 54.

46. Genesis 6:19-20, NIV.

47. http://www.pbs.org/wnet/nature/episodes/can-animals-predict-disaster/tall-tales-or-true/131/

48. Genesis 8:16-17, GNT.

49. Paul Taylor, www.answersingenesis.org/articles/nab/how-did-animals-spread#fnMark_1_4_1

6.
ARARAT: THE MOUNTAIN OF PAIN

50. http://www.noahsarksearch.com/ararat.htm

51. John Morris, *Adventure on Ararat*, quoted in Charles Berlitz, *The Lost Ship of Noah* (New York: G.P. Putnam's Sons, 1987), 70.

52. Mary Irwin, *The Unsolved Mystery of Noah's Ark*, (Bloomington, Indiana: Westbow Press, 2012), 10.

53. Charles Berlitz, *The Lost Ship of Noah*, 65-67.

54. Faustus of Byzantium

55. John Kitto, *Daily Bible Illustrations*, (London: Robert Carter & Bros., 1874), 160-163.

56. F.B. Lynch, *Armenia*, London, quoted by Violet M. Cummings, *Noah's Ark: Fable or Fact?* (Old Tappan, New Jersey: Fleming H. Revell, 1975), 19-20.

57. Tim F. LaHaye and John D Morris, *The Ark on Ararat* (Nashville: Thomas Nelson, Inc., Publishers, 1976), 31.

58. The recollection of Harold H. Williams, in LaHaye and Morris, *The Ark on Ararat*, 46.

59. Bob Cornuke and David Halbrook, *Lost Mountains of Noah*, (Nashville: Broadman & Holman Publishers), 9.

60. Ibid., 9.

61. Robert Cornuke, *Ark Fever*, (Wheaton, Illinois: Tyndale House Pulbishers, Inc.), 238.

62. Ibid., 245-6.

7.
ARKAEOLOGISTS: SEARCHING FOR THE ARK

63. Terry Wood, "The Search for Noah's Ark: Fact or Fable?" *The Plain Truth*, October, 1976, 24.

64. Violet M. Cummings, *Noah's Ark: Fable or Fact?* 83.

65. David Ballsiger and Charles Sellier, *Miraculous Messages: From Noah's Flood to the End Times*, (Alachua, Florida: Bridge-Logos Publishers, 2008), 263.

66. Fernand Navarra, *The Forbidden Mountain*, trans. Michael Legat (London: MacDonald, 1956), 130, quoted in LaHaye and Morris, *The Ark on Ararat,* 127.

67. Terry Wood, "The Search for Noah's Ark: Fact or Fable?" *The Plain Truth*, October, 1976, 25.

68. Terry Wood, "The Search for Noah's Ark: Fact or Fable?" *The Plain Truth*, October, 1976, 27.

69. http://creation.mobi/hong-kong-ark-fiasco

70. http://www.wnd.com/2010/04/146941/

8.
NOAH GOES TO HOLLYWOOD

71. Genesis 9:1, The Message.

72. *Noah's Ark* (1928) and its debt to DeMille, Peter T. Chattaway, June 11, 2007, http://www.patheos.com/blogs/filmchat/2007/06/noahs-ark-1928-and-its-debt-to-demille.html

73. http://godawa.com/movieblog/darren-aronofskys-noah-environmentalist-wacko/

9.
WHERE CAN YOU SEE THE ARK?

74. www.nydailynews.com/life-style/real-estate/dutchman-completes
-20-year-quest-build-full-scale-noah-ark-article-1.1217581

75. http://www.alpha.org.hk/eng/people/newcreation/thomaskwok.htm

76. http://gohongkong.about.com/od/whattoseeinhk/a/Noahs_Ark.htm

10.
NOAH'S SECRET FOR
SURVIVING THE END OF THE WORLD

77. Genesis 9:11, The Message.

78. Revelation 16:2-21, The Message.

79. Dan P. Lee, "Welcome to the Real Space Age," *New York Magazine*, May 27, 2013, 75.

80. Quoted on www.spacequotes.com from Edgar Mitchell, *The Way of the Explorer* (New Page Books, 2008).

81. Charles Siebert, "Food Ark," *National Geographic*, July, 2011, 116.

82. Bryan Walsh, "The Planet's Ultimate Backup Plan: Svalbard," *Time,* February 27, 2009.

83. www.regjeringen.no/en/archive/Stoltenbergs-2nd-Government/ Ministry-of-Agriculture-and-Food/Nyheter-og-pressemeldinger/ nyheter/2013/svalbard-global-seed-vault-secures-futur.html?id=715378

84. Bryan Christy, "Ivory Worship," *National Geographic*, October, 2012, 38.

85. www.theguardian.com/environment/2011/nov/27/orangutan -indonesia-endangered-species

86. Matthew 24:36-44, GNT.

87. www.Slashfilm.com, November 14, 2013
88. II Peter 3:3-7, The Message.
89. C.S. Lewis, *Mere Christianity*, (New York: HarperOne, 1952), 65.
90. Revelation 22:20-21, GNT.

LARRY STONE is an author—*The Story of the Bible* (Nelson) and *Women of the Bible* (Hudson)—and publisher. As vice president of Thomas Nelson Publishers and president of Rutledge Hill Press—a company best known for having published *Life's Little Instruction Book*—he has published more than a dozen *New York Times* bestsellers. A graduate of Moody Bible Institute and University of Iowa School of Journalism, Larry has studied at the New York University Graduate School of Business Administration, taught writing seminars in Africa, America, and the Caribbean, and has been executive director of KidShape, a non-profit that helps overweight children and their families become more healthy.

Larry is married to Lois and they have two sons—Brad and Geoff—and ten grandchildren. They are also "grandparents" to eleven others. They live in Nashville, Tennessee and Kattskill Bay, New York.

Thank you for choosing to read

NOAH: THE *REAL* STORY

If you enjoyed this book, we hope that you will tell your friends and family. There are many ways to spread the word:

Share your thoughts on Facebook, your blog, or Tweet "You should read #NOAHTHEREALSTORY by Larry Stone // @worldnetdaily
Consider using the book in a book group or small group setting. Send a copy to someone you know who would benefit from reading this book.

Write a review online at Amazon.com or BN.com
Subscribe to WND at www.wnd.com
Visit the WND Superstore at superstore.wnd.com

WND Books

A WND COMPANY   •   WASHINGTON DC   •   WNDBOOKS.COM

No publisher in the world has a higher percentage of *New York Times* bestsellers.

PRESENTS

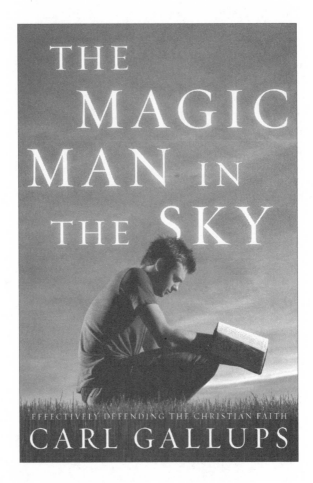

Are Christians just kidding themselves? Are believers wasting their lives serving an imaginary friend in the clouds? And do Christians even have the courage to confront the hard questions about God's existence? Carl Gallups does, and readers should be prepared for a gut-wrenching, exciting, and finally inspiring journey in his new blockbuster of Christian apologetics, *The Magic Man in the Sky.*

WND Books • A **WND** COMPANY • WASHINGTON DC • WNDBOOKS.COM

WND BOOKS

PRESENTS

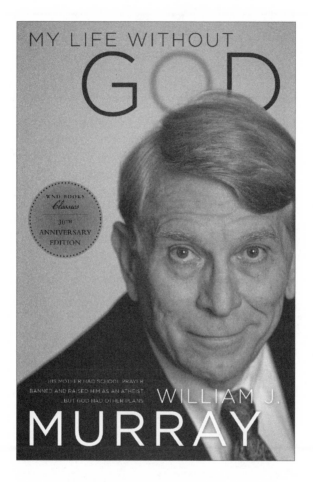

In 1963 America's most famous atheist, Madalyn Murray O'Hair, won the landmark
lawsuit filed on behalf of her son William, that effectively banned prayer in public schools.
From embezzlement to kidnapping to murder, Bill Murray reviews the shocking evidence
surrounding the disappearance of his mother, brother, and daughter. Though actively
involved in atheism, Bill discovered the gift Jesus Christ offers to all who seek Him.

WND BOOKS • A WND COMPANY • WASHINGTON DC • WNDBOOKS.COM